The Procrastination Cure (It's Not Eat That Frog!)

Blueprint to Master Time with Highly Effective Strategies to Solving the Productivity Puzzle and Rid Yourself of Laziness with Habits

Stephen N. Murphy

© Copyright 2019 - All rights reserved.

The content contained within this book may not be reproduced, duplicated or transmitted without direct written permission from the author or the publisher.

Under no circumstances will any blame or legal responsibility be held against the publisher, or author, for any damages, reparation, or monetary loss due to the information contained within this book. Either directly or indirectly.

Legal Notice
This book is copyright protected. This book is only for personal use. You cannot amend, distribute, sell, use, quote or paraphrase any part, or the content within this book, without the consent of the author or publisher.

Disclaimer Notice
Please note the information contained within this document is for educational and entertainment purposes only. All effort has been executed to present accurate, up to date, and reliable, complete information. No warranties of any kind are declared or implied. Readers acknowledge that the author is not engaging in the rendering of legal, financial, medical or professional advice. The content within this book has been derived from various sources. Please consult a licensed professional before attempting any techniques outlined in this book.

By reading this document, the reader agrees that under no circumstances is the author responsible for any losses, direct or indirect, which are incurred as a result of the use of information contained within this document, including, but not limited to, — errors, omissions, or inaccuracies.

Contents

Chapter 1:
The Reason You Procrastinate _____ 1

Chapter 2:
Productivity Secrets to Dominate _____ 14

Chapter 3:
The 10 Minute Rule Guaranteed to Work _____ 32

Chapter 4:
Fool Proof Method to Breaking Bad Habits _____ 38

Chapter 5:
Turn Procrastination into Motivation _____ 50

Chapter 6:
Time Management Strategies by Millionaires _____ 66

Chapter 7:
The Secret to Building Self-Discipline _____ 73

Chapter 8:
Essential Phrases to Stop Procrastinating _____ 93

Chapter 9:
The 5-Second Rule Mind Hack _____ 96

Chapter 10:
The Japanese Technique to Overcome Laziness _____ 100

Chapter 11:
3 Little-Known Techniques by Top Gurus _____ 105

Chapter 12:
How I Stopped Procrastinating (The #1 Method) _____ 108

Chapter 1:
The Reason You Procrastinate

One-fifth of the population procrastinates, and when you have such a negative impact on your life it diminishes your performance, affects your mental and physical health and increases your stress levels. This also makes you feel guilty and prolongs the timeframe you require to get tasks completed on a regular basis. It also affects the overall quality of the tasks. If you want to perform better and you do not want procrastination to affect the kind of work you do, it's important for you to find an effective solution.

There are several reasons why a person procrastinates, and it changes from person to person, which is why you need to first identify why you procrastinate in the first place. Once you identify the reason you procrastinate you will be able to work on it effectively and find the solution to a positive and healthy life.

You Lack Self-Compassion

If you do not have self-compassion, the tendency to stress always increases and this automatically increases the likelihood of procrastination.

People often wonder how they can suddenly introduce self-compassion to others. You can't! If you want to learn self-compassion you need to begin with yourself. Start talking kindly and motivate yourself even if you do something wrong. Instead of being a negative critic, start being positive and induce optimistic thoughts.

If you want to introduce self-compassion you must make sure that you practice forgiveness and stay open to the idea of forgiving yourself for the mistakes you make. Everyone makes mistakes in their life and at the end of the day you need to remind yourself that the mistakes you make are stepping stones towards learning on how to improve situations. Feeling bad about mistakes is not going to work well because this doesn't do you any good and it will only increase the chance of procrastination.

Always express gratitude because this is something that will ensure you introduce positive feelings inside of you and overcome your shortcomings as well. Gratitude is a great way to introduce self-compassion and is one of the most effective ways to teach yourself kindness as well. Generosity is another thing that will help increase self-compassion. The minute you become generous you start feeling positive and clear the clutter which gives you more space to think and take out the negativity from your life.

You Learned It from Someone

Procrastination is seldom self-taught which means you've either seen others behave in a particular manner and it has affected your ability to rationalize, or you've seen others demonstrate procrastination in front of you and learned to do the same, which is not healthy.

Sometimes you unknowingly latch on to information and behave in a particular manner. It's about learning how to unlearn what you realize is wrong. Positive people can bring about positive impacts in your life while negative people will make you feel low and sad. If you keep on thinking negative thoughts, then you won't manage to move on and teach yourself to become successful. You need to identify the root cause of your sorrows and why you keep feeling low so that you can work towards changing that and becoming a positive person. Procrastination has a lot to do with your emotions, and when you are emotionally drained or upset about something it becomes very difficult for you to feel good. This takes up most of your time and instead of planning how you will get things done you, you simply let the negativity take over your mind from time to time. This is not how you should function because it will eventually lead to self-destruction. Teach yourself to behave positively and find a role model who can teach you the right things.

You Underestimate Yourself

One of the major signs of procrastination is that you always underestimate yourself. While there is no clear explanation as to why people who procrastinate do this, they always do. Even if you're great at something, you will question your ability to be able to complete the task and start looking for the smallest errors once the task is complete. Some people don't even attempt doing something they could get done well because of procrastination.

Instead of trying to underestimate yourself you need to start motivating yourself and encourage yourself to do something you know you can attempt. Even if it turns out bad the first time, think about it as a learning experience and move on. Instead of feeling sorry for yourself you must learn and get better with each step you take. One of the root causes of procrastination is that you constantly believe you can't handle anything that you are asked to and no matter how hard you try you will deliver poor results, which is why people don't even try to attempt tasks that they could have done. Instead of underestimating yourself you need to teach yourself to get better.

You Can't Challenge Yourself

Unfortunately, one of the reasons you can't move ahead is because you continue to procrastinate. It's a never-ending cycle and until you learn how to break out of it, you may find yourself going around in circles.

The Procrastination Cure (It's Not Eat That Frog!)

If you want to overcome procrastination, it is important for you to continue challenging yourself and keep an open mind towards new things and accepting change. People who procrastinate are generally afraid of change and don't like to try new things since they believe they are not going to be good at it. Challenges are important for you to grow, and if you don't challenge yourself on a regular basis you will never manage to do well for yourself. One of the best ways to encourage yourself to try something new each day is to ensure you not only understand the importance of challenges but also how well they can work for you. While you may not want to challenge yourself at the start, once you do you will enjoy doing so, and this helps you get better at the things you do. Regularly challenging yourself also helps you to identify new ways to teach yourself something you never knew how to do. This is simple and effective, and it helps you get over procrastination. Challenges help you grow, and they are something you need to incorporate regularly to train your brain to get better and move higher up on the ladder of success.

Accurate Time Estimations

Most people procrastinate because they are not sure how long it will take to do certain tasks. Some people usually underestimate how quickly they can get things done and they often end up leaving work until the last minute. The main cause for this reason is overconfidence in your ability. Most people feel they will be able to manage tasks within a certain time frame even if they skip a couple of days in preparing for the task. This can come back to haunt you if the task turns out to be more difficult than you imagined or if it is something requires a lot of time to complete.

The best way to avoid this is to start earlier than planned and try to complete the task before the deadline. This will take care of any inaccurate time estimations and you can reward yourself with the time left on hand once you finish a task before schedule.

One of the major reasons for procrastination is that people end up with wrong time estimations, believing that they will be able to complete a job in no time at all. A realistic time frame is very important and without his time frame, not only will you end up delaying your tasks at hand, but you will also miss out on deadlines which will not leave a good impact on the person who is expecting the task complete from you. Proper time management is essential for you to move ahead and work towards success by overcoming procrastination. Don't underestimate how fast time flies because you need to manage it in the most effective way possible if you want a good and positive outcome.

Focusing on The Present Rather Than the Future
Most procrastination behaviors stem from the fact that people want their presence to be fruitful. People do not think too much about the future if they are able to procrastinate today. This usually results in quitting certain tasks if things become too difficult to handle.

The Procrastination Cure (It's Not Eat That Frog!)

You can avoid this by thinking about how your future can benefit from you working hard today. Getting an extra day to rest today is not really going to help you work harder and secure your future. You can't live for today, because at the end of the day if you don't plan your future you are not going to make your way to success. One of the most important things you need to remember when it comes to procrastinating is that if you live in the present without thinking about the future you won't be able to plan successfully, and you will constantly wonder if you have achieved anything. Planning is essential and without proper planning, you will not be able to achieve what you set out to do. Learn to plan your day effectively so you can use time more effectively, not just for the present but also for the future. After all, what you plan to create today can help you secure a better and more fruitful future.

Perfectionism

Another reason for procrastination is the importance of getting things done perfectly. This need for perfection often keeps you from starting work and this leads to delays and eventual failures to complete the work in hand.

Make sure you look back on your past examples where you have strived for perfection and not completed a task on time. This will give you enough motivation to complete tasks efficiently rather than perfectly. Stop trying to be perfect as it is impossible for you to perfect every task that you face. When you start targeting perfectionism it becomes difficult for you to stay focused on a task and get it completed effectively. No one will look solely for perfection in a task. What they look for is an effective result that can benefit them in the long run. Come up with solutions that will benefit you to save time and deliver more results rather than trying to perfect it. You won't be able to grow when you spend too much time on one particular task, but when you start handling multiple tasks you not only manage to expand your horizons but also grow as a person and become more successful. Focus on time management and efficiency rather than perfectionism.

Mental Illness Causing A Delay

Mental illnesses such as anxiety and depression can cause a delay in work. When you are suffering from depression or anxiety, you will not be able to focus on your work and your motivation will also likely be low.

Ensure treatment methods and therapy is incorporated into your life if you are not able to focus on work. If there are certain physical aspects that are causing your mood swings, you need to make sure you take care of those aspects before you start focusing on work again.

Procrastination is not easy to overcome but it is impossible to get over the tendencies of procrastination either. All you need to do is choose an effective path and have patience for it to work in your favor. There is no denying that procrastination limits your efforts to become productive, but it tricks you into feeling that this is not going to work, and you would only end up promising yourself things you never do. A smarter solution is to attempt small changes first and then go ahead with bigger changes once you have gotten used to the small changes you made. Through the process, you must keep motivating yourself and telling yourself that you can become better, more successful, and efficient in what you do by making simple changes in your life. Determination is important because motivation may not last forever, but determination will if you keep reminding yourself how important it is for you to stop procrastinating.

Dreadful Effects of Procrastination

People often underestimate how much procrastination can affect your life. If you were thinking that this is something you can deal with without having to struggle and without it affecting your regular day to day life, then you are sadly mistaken. Procrastination has a lot of negative effects on your life and when you learn to overcome them you will manage to see how much potential you have and what you can do with your goals by overcoming procrastination and focusing on success.

You Will Lose Precious Time

When you procrastinate on something you tend to put away any tasks that you have in hand irrespective of how close the deadline is. Instead of using time as your strength it becomes your biggest weakness because you wait until the last minute to get everything done and constantly regret it. Procrastination makes you feel low, and when you are in a negative state of mind it becomes difficult for you to turn that into something positive. A lot of people don't realize how much procrastination can affect you and they often think that they are simply getting distracted by certain scenarios in life and they need to deal with them before they can focus on work. The truth is that if you are procrastinating, something that is disturbing you today is more than likely to disturb you tomorrow, and even if that problem is sorted out it will keep coming up and you will still constantly be affected by it thereby making it difficult for you to work.

You Blow Off Opportunities

People look forward to an opportunity that can help them change their life, but unfortunately, they procrastinate and don't even realize these opportunities when they come knocking at their door because they are so busy complaining about the problems that they are going through. Most of the time, people don't even realize how they have given up on an opportunity because of ignorance and constant complaining. If you are always in a negative state of mind it will be very difficult for you to see something positive and you tend to ignore an opportunity that might be great for your career.

You Will Not Meet Your Goals

No matter how easy the task at hand is, people who procrastinate find it exceedingly difficult to keep up with their daily schedule and they always end up missing a deadline or delaying it. This is not because you have less time on hand. It is because you spent most of your time complaining. The worst thing about people that procrastinate is that it becomes difficult for them to identify the procrastination that's occurring regularly, and they only realize it when it's too late. Unless you have self-discipline implemented in your life you will not be able to realize how difficult it is for you to keep up with your daily tasks

It Could Ruin Your Career

People who procrastinate tend to snap because they are always in a negative mood and this doesn't benefit them because most of the time it works out against them. When you are constantly upset about things around you, you can't see the good in anyone or anything and this could put your job at risk because it makes it difficult for you to get along with the people you work with. Since you already delay your work and you are not able to keep up with the task at hand, there is a higher chance that you may end up losing the job because of your behavior. Procrastination generally ruins much more than you could even imagine and the sooner you identify the problem the more in control you will be and manage to take care of the situation.

It Lowers Your Self-Esteem

It lowers your self-esteem and makes you feel bad about yourself. Even if you are highly talented and skilled you will never be able to put your skill and talent to good use because you always feel that you are not worth it, and you will not be able to do anything effectively. The feeling of negativity usually grips you and you automatically believe that you aren't good at anything and no matter how hard you try you will not manage to achieve success. Ironically, people who procrastinate generally don't put in too much effort and although they believe they do, they do very little towards the job which is why they don't get it done as effectively.

Poor Decisions

When you are not in a proper frame of mind you will never manage to figure out what decisions are in favor of you and what are the kind of decisions you shouldn't take. Sometimes your decisions are even made just so that you can add stress upon yourself and see just to see how much emotional pressure you can handle. While a person who does not procrastinate will look towards taking a decision that will make them happy, people who procrastinate generally look to bring more sorrow into their life by making a tough choice.

Damage Your Reputation

People who procrastinate get labeled as being lazy and unable to get a job done on time. They also get labeled as being arrogant and annoying and people who do not get along with others that easily. While you may believe that this is your nature or the character that you have it's not so. it's because you are procrastinating, and you haven't realized it yet. Procrastination has a lot of negative effects on your life and the sooner you identify these problems the easier it will be for you to deal with them. There is a cure for everything and once you know that you are procrastinating you can work towards treating it effectively.

You Risk Your Health

People who procrastinate tend to spend most of their time doing almost nothing and then become lethargic and lazy. It also increases their stress and anxiety levels, and this causes various problems including increased risk of depression. People who procrastinate may get depressed because of their inability to complete tasks and this usually is a reason why they may spend time alone. Being alone can put them at high risk to succumb to various other mental illnesses. Depression can potentially ruin your life and unless you do something to work towards treating it you will not be able to lead a productive life.

If you do not want procrastination to take over your life, it's important for you to identify you are procrastinating and take the necessary measures to work towards fighting it.

Chapter 2:
Productivity Secrets to Dominate

Procrastination is not easy to overcome which is why a lot of people struggle with it for a long time. If you want to overcome procrastination you got to identify your skills and enhance them the right way so that you can convert your weaknesses into your strengths and start benefiting from it. People often wonder how they can overcome procrastination and what needs to be done in order to do so. I will let you in on some effective secrets that work well to overcome procrastination and lead you on the path of success.

Empty Your Mind

It is important for you to clear up physical clutter so that you will be able to work more effectively or do something productive - it's the same with your mind. If there are a lot of thoughts in your head, this won't help you in any way and it will make it tough to focus on one topic because there so many things going on in your head. For you to begin your journey against procrastination, you need to learn how to control what you think about and prioritize your thoughts. It may sound silly, but some people end up procrastinating over the smallest things and waste time complaining instead of doing something about it. You need to understand there are two situations in life - the ones you can control and the ones you can't. Here's what you need to remember - you are only in control of your thoughts and no matter how much you would like to change the way a person thinks about you or what they say about you, it's not in your hands. Instead of worrying about what people have to say, try diverting that energy into doing something beneficial for yourself. Stressing about situations you can't control makes no sense because it will make you feel bad and you will continue procrastinating. The best way to get back at people who talk about you or make you feel bad about yourself is to complete something and become successful. If you want to do that, you need to start by clearing your thoughts and prioritizing what's important and making your mind sharper.

Have a day just to yourself

This benefits you a great deal because it helps you think effectively without disturbing you in any way. You are what you need to do. Have one day during the week where you avoid doing any tasks at all. If you sit down to work and you notice that you often get distracted by your cellphone or social media networking sites, make it a point to not use those gadgets or websites for one day. This doesn't mean you start living off the grid and avoid your phone completely. While you can use your phone to make phone calls when necessary, stop scrolling through the messages or using it for other purposes other than calls.

If you are addicted to talking to people over the phone, have a time limit on the number of phone calls as well as the duration of the calls during that free day. What this does is it helps you to stay focused and stops you from getting sidetracked by unnecessary activities that eat into your time in which you could have invested in doing something beneficial and fruitful for yourself. It's not easy to give up something you are addicted to which is why you should set one day aside to fulfill your needs so that you motivate yourself towards working hard and getting one step closer to success. You must remember that success comes at a price and it isn't easy to get. The more effort you put, the higher the rewards you reap.

Prioritize Your Work

While the first step in prioritizing your work is to clear your mind and ensure that you only focus on what is important, you need to spend the time to sort out work based on what is more important or less important. There are very repetitive tasks that you will have to do daily, and these will be your regular tasks which you have to get done. If you want to make the most out of your time, then you should try to finish up your regular tasks faster so you have more time on hand as well as energy to focus on important tasks that can help you become successful. There are many things on which you will waste time on a regular basis, and you may want to figure out where you are investing that time so you will be able to cut down on the distractions and prioritize more effectively. Prioritizing your tasks also helps you identify where you are eating up into your time and how small changes in your routine you can give you more time to focus on becoming successful. When you prioritize your time and there's an important task, you can focus on it more effectively and this means that you are putting in quality as well as quantity towards the task, thereby increasing the chances of being highly successful.

Break Down Your Time

Instead of working consistently for a long period of time, you need to try to break down your tasks into multiple sections that are no longer than 15 to 20 minutes each. After each successful completion of a task you can move on to the next. With this method you can then focus on small portions of the bigger task and ensure that you get them done well. 15 minutes seems like a short amount of time to get work done, but you start focusing more effectively. This helps to increase your productivity without putting too much stress on you. It is also important for you to take a break in between your work session which means if you have 3 back-to-back tasks you should give yourself one break before you resume the fourth task. This not only helps you in terms of energy, it helps you to calm your mind and focus as you did on the first task. Time management is very important when it comes to beating procrastination but it's important for you to realize it takes time. Make it a habit to break down certain tasks into multiple portions so you can make better use of time.

Choose Your Thinking Position or Place

There are a lot of people who manage to think better when they are in a place or position. Instead of limiting yourself to your office desk you should see where you are most comfortable and where you feel most relaxed. That is probably the place you will be most creative and be able to think and brainstorm for the best ideas that can benefit you and help you become successful.

Maintain an Unlimited to Do List

Almost everyone has a to-do list, and sometimes this list gets so lengthy it is impossible for you to keep up with the never-ending task list. While it's good to have a to-do list, it's important for you to prioritize that list and mark tasks based on whether they are less important or more important. Always begin with the ones that are most important or have restricted time frames so you can focus on the other less important tasks with the remaining time you have left. You should prepare a to-do list in such a way that the tasks that are important should be completed during the day you receive it and the least important ones can be left for other days. It's all about finding your rhythm - where you decide what must be done at the start of the day when you have the most energy and where you are more focused, and what can be left for the end of the day that doesn't require too much of your attention. Practical thinking always works because if you want to become successful you need to make practical decisions by keeping in mind tasks that will benefit you.

Don't Pressure Yourself

The Procrastination Cure (It's Not Eat That Frog!)

Let's face it; we all have so much to do yet so little time that it can be daunting. It's important for you to draw a line every day and decide that this is how much work you can handle and nothing more. When you take up too much work or more work than you can handle it affects your productivity and quality of work, which means it will take you nowhere. There is a difference between working smarter and working harder which is why you need to limit the amount of work you do based on your ability to cope and the time you have. Sometimes a task could be completed in less than 2 hours, but it could drain you out of your energy completely which means you need to rest before you start a new task, especially if you want to get it done just as well as you did the previous task. Just because something can be completed in 2 hours doesn't mean you take up multiple such jobs for an 8-hour work schedule. Remember, you need to account for break time too. Most of these tasks will be done during your peak hours and it will be the cause of low energy levels and lack of focus. Breaks are important and you have to consider the amount of time your body takes to relax and rejuvenate before you get back to work so you can maintain quality.

Make A Daily Action Plan

Your to-do list doesn't have to be everything that you do daily; there can always be something spontaneous on your agenda. This could be anything from treating yourself after a well-worked week or challenging yourself to do a little more on a Monday just see you how much you can push yourself. You need to remember that your daily actions that may or may not be successful, but that doesn't have to disrupt your routine. You simply need to change the way you think and approach the situation. It's something that can help you better yourself or figure out what needs to be changed and whether there is room for improvement.

Prioritize the Difficult Projects First

When you start your day, you need to make sure that you prioritize your work and note it down based on urgency and difficulty. If there are many tasks to complete that don't require a lot of time to complete, then you should start with the most difficult tasks first. Once the worst is out of the way it will give you enough time to complete the rest of the tasks that are relatively easier, and you will have less stress as well. Prioritizing not only helps you complete all the tasks at hand, but it will also ensure that you think with a clear mind and do not handle too many tasks at the same time. Starting with these later and keeping the difficult ones for the end of the day will make your day extremely difficult. You will continue dreading the moment when the difficult tasks need to be completed and this will keep you demotivated throughout the day.

Two-Minute Rule

The two-minute rule was introduced by none other than David Allen. This rule is extremely simple. When you are handed a task, take a moment to figure out whether it can be completed within 2 minutes or not. If it can be completed in two minutes, then you should do it immediately. This will reduce the length of your task list and it will take a lot off your plate once you start implementing this properly. The only flipside to this rule is you should not start doing tasks in two minutes just for the heck of it. If a task requires time, make sure you give it ample time and do justice to the work that has been assigned to you. The way this works is that it helps you to work in small intervals and this keeps you motivated throughout. You tend to get more done when you look at work in two-minute intervals and it helps you be more productive. When there are a ton of small and minor jobs that need to get done, you will manage to complete them without any delays or procrastination because in a mere two minutes there's not a lot of time left for you to think. It's like a constant challenge where you push yourself to finish multiple tasks during the day. While these small tasks don't seem like much, when they accumulate it tends get to you and you feel pressurized to finish them. The two-minute rule helps you knock the small tasks out of the way systematically and leaves only the big tasks pending.

Assign A Work Area

If you work in an office, it goes without saying that you would have a cubical that would be assigned to you and you would be expected to work from this space. If you work from home, then you need to make sure that you segregate your work life from your personal life. It can be very easy to sit on the couch and write if you work from home, but this will compromise the integrity of the task at hand and you will not be able to complete it accurately. Even when you work from home you need to make sure that you assign a workspace and that space should be used only for your work and nothing else. Your comfort level is important while you work but it does not mean that you get so comfortable that you end up procrastinating and taking a quick power nap.

One of the worst things you can do when you work from home is to plonk yourself on the bed to work. Sitting on your bed with your laptop is the least productive way to get things done since you'll never feel like you're working. When you work you've got to put your energy into focusing on the task and this can't be done in a casual place, like your bed, where you rest and relax most of the time. It's all about creating the right mindset in order to get more work done.

If you work from home, you should always take the time to build your own workspace. This needs to be a separate space and should in no way be connected to your comfort zone or the space you spend time relaxing. You also need to make sure this space is not too close to the television or other recreational activities such as your gaming console or even your mp3 player. Having these distractions close to your workspace is a strong temptation and when you look at these gadgets, you'll feel like utilizing them. When you work, you need to stay focused on what you do and the only way you'll be able to do this is when you stay away from these distractions. When it's out of sight, it's usually out of your mind too. So, try to keep these distractions out of your sight when you're working.

Peak Working Hours

When you work a 9 to 5 schedule, there would be certain hours of the day that you would be most productive and other times that you would not deliver as much work as expected. The same would be the case when you are working from home. If you feel that 9 to 5 is not your cup of tea, then you could decide your golden hours for work and work according to that schedule. There are people that work from home and sleep through the day while working at night. This helps keep away all the distractions and they can work peacefully. Some people even start their work in the afternoon and end up working until late in the evening. No matter what schedule you stick to, you need to make sure that you are alert during that time, and you cross maximum things off your list. Once you have decided your peak working hours you need to make sure that you stick to that and not change your schedule too often.

Figuring out what time you're most productive is key. If you haven't figured it out yet, take time to try working at odd hours for a few days and see the time you found most comfortable to work. There are several people who aren't aware about the hours they are most productive at and often stumble upon it by accident. If you want to learn about your golden hours, you need to stretch your work hours for a few days to figure it out.

Eliminate Distractions

If you need to complete certain tasks within a limited time frame then you may want to eliminate all distractions in your work environment. One of the biggest distractions these days is the internet. If you just need to sit down and write, then you may want to pretend that you are in an airplane and the internet connectivity is very limited. You should also pretend that your cell phone does not function. This will allow you to work without any kind of interruption and it will keep you very focused.

Putting your phone away can help increase productivity by a great extent. Not only does it allow you to focus better, you end up saving a ton of time and manage to get the job done faster when your phone is away.

Be Consistent

The key to success is always staying on top of your game and continuing to work as soon as you finish the previous task. The most successful writers in the world started writing their new book as soon as they finished their previous one. They don't wait to read feedback they receive for the book because they believe in their work, so they continue writing. Successful writers make it a point to write a minimum of 2000 words daily. This keeps the creativity flowing and it also ensures that the work never stops. When you work continuously, the momentum will be in your favor.

The Procrastination Cure (It's Not Eat That Frog!)

When you're not consistent with what you do, you end up with different results for each day. This means you won't be able to judge whether you're delivering the kind of work you want. You don't have to push yourself to your limits every day. When you have a schedule planned and when you stick to it, you will end up being more productive without struggling to meet deadlines and without having to stay up for long hours.

Take Care of Your Health

While you may feel that you need to work all the time and not take any breaks, you should make sure that you do not experience burn out. The endeavor to be successful should not be so fierce that you end up falling ill. Take enough breaks through the day and take at least one day off during the week. This will not only help protect your body, but it will also protect your frame of mind.

If you want to perform well, you've got to stay healthy and look after yourself. If you're not healthy, you'll end up missing out on a few days of work and this will hinder your progress along with your commitment to staying consistent. Try to give yourself a break every now and then. Always remember, the minute you feel the pressure is getting to you, relax. The key to performing well long term is to understand when you need to stop for a while before you resume the task at hand.

Try Various Methods

If you have been working hard and you are not getting the right kind of results, then you need to try and change your working style. What may have worked for someone else will not necessarily work for you. Always look to innovate with your work and do something different daily. When your working style becomes monotonous, it will reflect in the results. Changing your working methods regularly will ensure you always stay excited about your work and have different methods to work with each time.

Living by the book may not be the best solution for everyone. While a few things work well for some, it might not be the best solution for another. It may take you awhile to find something that works, so keep experimenting with different methods until you find your mojo and once you do, stick to it.

Procrastination is more common than you can imagine and due to this, there are several misconceptions that are related to how you should be able to overcome procrastination effectively. If you want to increase self-discipline and you want to walk the path of success, you need to make sure you differentiate between what is myth and what will work. Here are a few myths that you should not believe regarding procrastination.

#1 - I Work Better Under Pressure
Pressure seldom brings out the best in you and while you may create an illusion that you are working really hard and efficiently because

you are pressured for time, the truth is that you will end up making a lot of mistakes because you want to get the job done faster rather than more efficiently. While there are a few people who tend to work well under pressure, this isn't something one should do regularly since it takes a toll on your health. While working under pressure may help you get the kind of results you're aiming for, you won't be able to pull this off for long. Working under pressure will drain you out and you will eventually get tired. This will start affecting your overall productivity and you won't be able to keep up to the growing demands of your work.

When under pressure, you try working faster on a task and there's a possibility you will try to cut the job short and take shortcuts. This may not work out to benefit the project. It all begins when you start procrastinating and delaying work, leaving it all until the last minute. Procrastination will harm your overall performance and it won't help you to perform better because pressure leads to stress and stress leads to silly mistakes that will be reflected in your work.

Don't convince yourself that you do well under pressure, instead convince yourself to work well in a systematic way where there is no pressure and where you enjoy doing what you do. It is important for you to remember that enjoying what you do matters more than anything because that's when you start doing work that is good quality and will get you credit for. Pressure doesn't do that.

#2 - I Need Inspiration to Work

You may not have inspiration every day of your life, but you still must work every day if you want to get closer to your goal. You can't just wait to 'get in the mood' but rather you must create the mood and motivate yourself to work well every day.

You also need to tell yourself not all days are the same and you may feel great on certain days but that there are days that may not be that well-organized and there will be times you may get frustrated or upset. However, that's not the reason for you to stop working, but rather for you to push yourself and remind yourself that you should work because you have a stipulated time frame and an agenda you have to stick to, rather than letting the day go to waste just because of negative emotions.

You can't expect others to inspire you all the time and while you can try to change circumstances a little and create a more positive work environment it begins from within you. You must be the source of your inspiration rather than depending on anybody else to be that for you. Inspiring yourself is easier than having to depend on another person to do so and it also gets you more in control of your emotions which means you will be able to take control of the tasks in hand and not let your feelings affect the outcome.

#3 - Needing Three or Four Hours of Uninterrupted Time

The Procrastination Cure (It's Not Eat That Frog!)

This is a very common myth that several people use as an excuse in order to delay work that is being done by them. There are several ways that you can stop procrastination and do a lot of work in very little time. You need to save little chunks of time from various other tasks and then use the chunks together to complete a difficult or a massive task. It is very difficult to find large chunks of time available if you lead a very busy life. Waiting for a large portion of uninterrupted time is just an excuse to procrastinate your work because you know that chunk is not going to be available. If you keep waiting until the last minute you will then pressure yourself to complete the task quickly and before you know it, you will end up performing poorly.

There are several rules that you can follow in order to get difficult tasks completed well within the time frame. You need to use these rules to your advantage. One of the things you can do is use the Swiss cheese approach in order to break down large tasks. If you have seen a Swiss piece of cheese you will know that there are several holes in it - this is what you need to get done with your tasks. Poke small holes into your tasks and reduce the demands of the task over a period. The small holes could be in the form of time that you take out from your busy schedule to complete a portion of that big task. The biggest fear that people have is starting a task and not realizing the sheer volume of the task. Once you have begun working on a task, you will realize that the task was not as difficult as you expected it to be. When you start poking holes into a task you will make constant progress and you will end up finishing the task with ease.

You need to make use every minute that you have when you have a busy schedule. If you have 30 minutes to spare after your lunch hour, you can ask yourself what can be done within that time frame. Do not look at your task as a large chunk of work that needs to be completed. When you break down your tasks in two portions, you will be able to finish it one bit at a time with the small chunks of time that you have been able to spare throughout your day.

#4 - I Will Do A Better Job Later

Yes, we all have made this mistake of thinking that tomorrow is going to be a better day. How often do we procrastinate because we were just too scared to take up tasks today? It is very easy to sit down and think that tomorrow you will be able to do a better job because you will be better organized, and you will have more control over the tasks. However, the truth remains that unless you start doing a task today you will not be productive tomorrow. If you were running short on time today, you will run out of time tomorrow as well. If you are not disciplined today, you will never be disciplined anytime soon. Start pushing yourself and get work done today. Yes, it will take a little bit of effort and it will need a little bit of coaxing from within, but you need to get it done. Avoid using this excuse because this is one of the worst procrastination myths and you will never get out of this vicious cycle. Your proposed tomorrow will never come, and you will never be able to complete any of the tasks that you have to do.

Most of us use some or all these myths on a daily basis and we continue delaying the tasks that we have. Just because a task makes you feel uncomfortable, it doesn't mean you need to be afraid of it. Sometimes even a complex task can turn out to be one of the easiest ones on your list. Don't be overwhelmed by the things that you do because if you do not do the task, someone else will. If you want to move ahead in life and be successful, you cannot let others take over your responsibilities as this will not put you in a good light. Stop putting yourself down and be confident in your ability to work on important and difficult tasks. It's time to kick these myths out the window.

Chapter 3:
The 10 Minute Rule Guaranteed to Work

Several people tend to put off tasks that cause them physical discomfort or emotional discomfort and that's when they begin procrastination. It could be as small as not wanting to talk to somebody over the phone or planning a daily schedule that you are forced to follow. Although most people believe that getting over procrastination is a tough task, the truth is you need to make the right decisions and stay determined to do so. The 10-minute rule is something that a lot of people believe works very well to overcome procrastination, and this is something I back completely. It's easy to follow, simple, and highly effective.

How to Use The 10-Minute Rule?

The 10-minute rule is simple, all you need to do is tell yourself that you are going to focus on working on a task uninterrupted for 10 minutes. Once you reach the 10-minute mark you will ask yourself again whether you want to keep going for another 10 minutes and continue if you decide you want to. At the end of the 10 minutes when you question yourself about continuing the task or not, you will end up continuing for at least 9 of those times you challenge yourself. This means that without forcing yourself to get something done, you will manage to increase productivity in an effective way.

The 10-minute rule is a great way to overcome procrastination and push yourself to work a little more each time. When you convince yourself to work for 10-minutes, you end up feeling good in the process and you automatically want to do more once you start. This not only helps you to work more consistently, but also more efficiently.

Why This Rule Works

Most people stress about getting a short task done and dread the moment they need to start the task. The 10-minute rule allows you to work for 10 minutes at a time, which will make the total time seem like a small amount of time to invest in. You can decide whether you want to continue with another 10-minute task at the end of the 10th minute and so on. This illusion of working for just 10 minutes motivates you to work and you start immersing yourself in the task without realizing how many hours go by.

The 10-minute rule helps you to focus on tasks that you aren't even interested in doing and ensure that you get it done in an effective way. It helps you to overcome the negative feelings and the feelings of anxiety that you normally go through when you are not confident about starting a task.

Convince yourself that you need to invest only 10 minutes in doing something you started with a positive mindset, and once you start performing the task you are motivated to finish it. Doing this on a regular basis will not only help increase productivity, but it also improves the quality of work that you deliver thereby getting you a little closer to success. When you incorporate the 10-minute rule into your daily life you start eliminating procrastination completely.

It's All About Getting Started

Before you begin, all you need to do is ask yourself whether you are ready to challenge yourself for the next 10 minutes, and before you know it, you will manage to do it effectively. Here are three steps that will come handy in implementing the 10-minute rule:

Delegate Work

Delegation has been the most successful way of managing work and time. There are certain managers that are excellent at what they do, and they never seem to say no to any task assigned to them. Delegation has several benefits and you need to make sure that you use this method to the fullest. When you start assigning work to others, your to-do list will keep decreasing and you will have ample time to focus on the important tasks at hand. This is where the 10-minute rule can be implemented excellently. Take a moment to study your to-do list and make sure that you delegate all the tasks that can be completed within 10 minutes. This will help you complete all tasks within the deadline and ensure that you are doing so without any stress.

Delegated work may sound easy, but it is not. There are times when you end up not delegating a certain task because you are not sure how the other person will deliver. You need to remember one simple rule - completing a task well is better than completing it perfectly. There will always be imperfections, even in your own work. The only way you can succeed is by moving ahead and letting go of things. When you start delegating work you will be able to take on additional responsibilities and new projects. This will help you learn and grow in your career. If you continue doing the same tasks daily you will never progress, and you will remain at an entry-level position. If you are looking to get promoted, you need to find somebody that can do your current job. If you are irreplaceable at your current job, the management will never promote you because they feel that no one else can do the tasks that you are currently doing. Delegating will show that you are capable of trusting others and you will be interested in taking up more responsibilities by higher management.

Break Up the Tasks

You should know that almost every task can be broken up into 10-minute microtasks. This will help you complete a two-hour task in just 30 minutes. For example, you need to come up with a new plan to improve sales in your organization. You can break this task up into several 10-minute microtasks. Take the first 10 minutes and figure out how you can get new ideas. Once you have jotted down new ideas, you can take another 10 minutes and log on to the internet to try and elaborate on these ideas. Once that is done, take another 10 minutes and get everyone gathered near your desk for a brainstorming session. While the brainstorming session may not be completed within 10 minutes, you have completed the planning phase of the task at hand in less than an hour and this is how a 10-minute rule can prove to be effective to you.

The 10-minute rule can also be implemented in your personal life. If you have been reaching the office late daily, you need to figure out your morning routine and see what can be changed. Break down all your morning tasks into 10 minutes and this will help you get organized a lot quicker. Try brushing your teeth and washing your face in 10 minutes, taking a shower in 10 minutes, eating your breakfast in 10 minutes and gathering all your things together to leave the house in 10 minutes. These are some of the major tasks that you carry out in the morning and all of it can be completed in less than an hour. This is the power of the 10-minute rule.

Use A Timer
Several people try to implement the 10-minute rule however they fail because they lose track of time and 10 minutes turn into 2 hours. When you are in a high-stress situation at work, time can fly, and you need to make sure that you stick to the 10-minute rule in order to make time your best friend. always Keep a timer with you - these days it is very easy because almost every smartphone has an inbuilt timer.

The Procrastination Cure (It's Not Eat That Frog!)

Time each of your tasks that you are striving to complete under 10 minutes and see where you are falling behind.

The only way you can maximize productivity is by pushing yourself and trying to complete tasks within the allotted time frame. While certain tasks may go beyond 10 minutes, you should not let it linger on until you lose complete track of time and do not complete the task at all. Keeping track of time will help you improve over a period and you will become a lot more efficient. At the end of the day, you need to keep experimenting with the various time frames that work best for you and stick to the 10-minute rule. You may not be able to be as motivated as you want to the first time, but the secret is to just keep going until you find your rhythm and manage to use it to your advantage.

Chapter 4:
Fool Proof Method to Breaking Bad Habits

Procrastination can cause you to delay a lot of your tasks because of the feeling of laziness and putting off things on your to-do list until the end of the day. If you want to overcome procrastination, it's important that you do the right thing and learn how to break habits that hamper your efficiency. You also need to understand that it's not something which will happen within a few days but rather something that needs effort, invested time, as well as determination for you to figure out the most effective ways to be productive and overcome procrastination. There is a lot that you can do to achieve better results within the same time frame. It all involves using methods that work well for you and understanding the importance of making the most out of your time rather than spending it worrying about whether you will be able to get something done on time.

Breaking the Task into Smaller Steps
One of the major reasons people procrastinate is because they find it extremely difficult to get the job done since it seems too overwhelming to complete. While some tasks are small, others may require you to invest a lot of time and the fear of having to deal with

such a big project may lead you to procrastinate. Instead of pondering over how you're going to accomplish a big task, it makes more sense for you to break it down into smaller portions so that you don't need to look at it is a big project.

Let's take the example of writing a book and break it down into phrases that will make it easy for you to complete the task at hand. You could include the following phases:

- Research
- Narrowing down the topic
- Creating an outline
- Drafting the content
- Writing the chapters
- Proofreading
- Adding the final touches

When you break down your work into smaller portions it seems to be more manageable and you are more able to get the job done on time. Once you have broken down your work into smaller portions you then need to dedicate time and ensure that you get everything done in your stipulated time frame, so you do not delay the project. Give yourself a realistic time frame so you don't end up getting things done last minute. It benefits you in the number of ways because it not only helps you to focus better but you end up delivering quality work that you will be proud of.

Change Your Environment

This may surprise you but different environments have different impacts regarding your productivity. If you suddenly feel demotivated in your workspace or when you are at home, try thinking about places that you believe will motivate you to do better. You can also experiment with new places where your productivity is at its peak. For some writers, coffee shops could be a great place to put on your thinking cap and come up with innovative ideas to write about. When you confine yourself to a space you don't allow yourself to unleash and think, and this leads to eventual procrastination. Sometimes when you spend too much time at home, the feeling of laziness starts to creep up and each time you look at your bed you may want to snuggle in and go for a quick nap. All of this can be avoided if you think smart and figure out places where you manage to work most effectively. If you like sitting in the library, try and spend as much time as you can there because it's one of the most effective places for you to focus on work. Libraries are quiet, there are no distractions, and you cannot talk which means you won't be distracted in any way and you will put in all your energy on work.

You can also head to a coffee shop to work. While you may think such a place would have a lot of distractions, it helps you relax and get creative. If you're used to a coffee shop, make it a point to visit the same one. There's something about familiar places that help you work better. If you haven't discovered your space yet, you need to explore the possible options that you think could work well for you. However, don't spend your day shifting from one coffee shop to another. If you think this will not work for you, try another alternative such as a library.

Create Your Own Deadlines

As mentioned in point one you should always dedicate a certain amount of time to each task and set a realistic deadline so you know you must have that task completed by that date. When you have too much work to handle but there are a lot of days before the deadline, you tend to take it easy for the first few days because you are not close to the deadline and psychologically you tend to believe you have enough time before you need to start your task. Unfortunately, people find it difficult to stick to deadlines because they avoid working for a few days and this creates a lot of stress. If you want to avoid all of this, you need to remember that apart from breaking down your tasks into smaller and easier jobs you also need to set deadlines for each task. If a task is relatively easy then give yourself a day or two to finish it, and if it's a little more difficult try assigning 3 to 4 days for you to finish the job. If the work requires about 15 to 20 days always give yourself at least two days off and during these two days make sure to pamper yourself so you are rejuvenated and motivated to get back to work.

Promise yourself that you will only take a day off when you complete a certain number of tasks on your list, so you know you are at par with your timeline. The final deadline that you pick should be at least a day prior to the actual deadline date because it's always important to give yourself a buffer and a little wiggle room.

In case something goes wrong or there's an emergency you need to tend to, you'll still manage to get the job done on time because of the buffer you gave yourself. If you finish the task before the actual deadline, you can always use the spare day to pamper yourself or relax. After all, you need to rest before you take on a new task if you want to continue performing well.

Eliminate Distractions
While some people tend to procrastinate when they are stressed, others procrastinate a little more frequently. If you realize you are procrastinating way too much and you are not able to focus on a task even after you are breaking it down and assigned it time, then you need to eliminate distractions and force yourself to focus. You need to eliminate all external distractions including your social media pages that you browse in between work hours and use a filter to block the sites or deactivate your accounts until you complete your tasks. While most people manage to take control over procrastination by

setting certain deadlines and tasks that they should do on days, if you are unable to do that, then taking a drastic step may help you to focus and get back on track. Instead of deactivating your social media accounts, you can always ask a trustworthy friend to change your passwords and give them to you only after you have completed a certain number of tasks. This will help you motivate yourself to get the job done fast and without distractions and it becomes a lot easier for you to focus. Eliminating distractions is not difficult, what's difficult is to take the first step towards eliminating it because we are so dependent and addicted to these websites. Once you absorb yourself in work, you will not feel the need to go to the websites repeatedly and you manage to focus more on work and put your energy where it matters.

Hangout with People Who Inspire You

Try and stay away from bad influences. When you spend time with people who influence in a negative way you procrastinate. Similarly, when you spend time with people who have a positive impact on your life you start performing better because you are motivated to do well. When you look at highly successful people and what they have accomplished in their life you realize that it doesn't come easy. One of the most important things that they invested in was effort and long hours of unrestricted work. If you want to see yourself in their position or anywhere close to it, you must follow their footsteps and do things that makes you more productive rather than force you to procrastinate. A positive mindset has a positive impact on your life, and it will help you live a more fulfilling life that benefits you. You'll always have negative people in your life that will tell you to spend time doing things that won't benefit you in any way, but if you want to become successful, you must work hard and eliminate distractions including bad influences from your life.

It's shocking how much people can influence you and this doesn't just have to do with major distractions. It could even be something as small as forcing you to abandon your task to head out for a smoke break or just to engage in unnecessary gossip. While it's important for you to socialize, you need to know whom to socialize with and how much time you should invest in socializing. You should also consider spending time with people who inspire rather than annoy you. Make sure you spend time discussing ideas, not people.

Great Minds Discuss Ideas. Average Minds Discuss Events. Small Minds Discuss People. Personal Excellence.

Find A Friend or Companion

The one thing that will motivate you to work effectively and enjoy what you do is having a friend or a companion who shares the same interests and goals as you. When you have somebody to encourage you, not only do you manage to achieve your goals a lot faster, but you manage to execute a plan more effectively. It also helps you to assist each other during difficult times, and it manages to lift your spirit and brings you back on track. When you spend time with somebody who works with you, energy levels are always high, and this automatically brings out the best in the both of you. You can also learn how to delegate tasks together and come up with the most effective solutions to work towards achieving the goal as a team. When you have a partner, who has the same goals as you, you convert your work time to fun time and start enjoying what you do.

Tell Others About Your Goal

It's very important for you to let people know what you are doing and how proud you are of it. Whether it's your family members, your friends, colleagues, or even acquaintances, make sure you let them know about the project that you have taken up and just how motivated you are towards working and completing it on time. While you don't have to boast about how well you are doing, simply inform them about how motivated you are to get work done because not only will this convince you of your motivation levels but it will make you feel proud each time you talk about it and this will encourage you to work harder. Acknowledging what you do lessens procrastination and makes you more confident in doing the job. For you to be able to overcome feelings of anxiety or procrastination you have to be confident with your skills. One of the best ways to do it is to continuously talk about your plans and how you are going to execute them in a more effective way. When you talk about your goals don't worry about what other people say, just focus on letting them know what you plan to do. You also need to decide who you want to stop sharing information with.

Sometimes people tend to put you down and if you get a feeling of negativity from somebody every time you try to tell him about your goal you may want to refrain from telling these people because they will only make you feel bad about yourself and you will begin procrastinating again.

Talk to Someone Who Has Achieved A Lot

As stated above, if you want to make the most out of your life you need to have a role model who inspires you and guides you in the right direction. This doesn't necessarily mean it has to be somebody who is a millionaire or is very rich but someone who is happy with life and content with what they have achieved. You must also remind yourself that success isn't only measured in terms of money but also in terms of how much somebody has done and how content they are with their life. You should look for someone you believe has achieved almost everything you would want and look up to them as a role model. Open and communicate with them so you can get ideas on how you should plan your goals and your life ahead. When you look up to somebody in a positive way and seek advice from them you can always ask for solutions that can help you become a better person.

Recheck Your Goals After A While

If you're haven't procrastinated for a while and you believe that you are getting better at being productive, then it's time for you to check on your goals and see how well you are doing. If it's getting too easy to complete tasks and you have a lot of spare time you may want to think about how you want to dedicate more time to performing better. At the end of the day, it is all about getting closer to your dream and becoming more focused towards success than ever before.

The more time you spend following the right ways to break from the habit of procrastination, the better you'll get, and this simply means that you should also challenge yourself a little more every time. After all, it's important for you to grow, and for you to do this, you must take a bigger step ahead every few months.

You should also set long term goals for yourself and recheck every few months to see whether you are achieving those goals or whether you have gotten any closer to them than you were a few months ago. When you get a certain amount of your goals achieved you should pamper yourself by giving yourself a day off, taking a holiday, or even buying something nice for yourself. It is important to reward yourself for the good work you do because that keeps you motivated to keep doing better so you can provide for yourself and for your family.

Don't Over Complicate Things

One of the worst habits of people who procrastinate is that they over-complicate things by continuously trying to make them better. You need to understand that perfectionism is not something you can achieve all the time, and your work doesn't have to be perfect, it just needs to be done efficiently. There is a huge difference between perfectionism and efficiency and the reason people procrastinate is because they aim for perfection over efficiency. For you to be successful you don't need to be perfect you just need to get the job done in a timely manner.

The key to living a happy life is to live a simple life. The more you complicate matters the more problems you create for yourself. You've got to come to terms with the fact that you can either do something about a problem or you can't. If you can, instead of complaining get up and do it, and if you can't it's best to let it go.

Stop Complaining
The number one habit of procrastination is complaining - the minute you break this habit you will become a better person. You are never going to have everything your way. There is always going to be a reason to complain. You just need to learn when to stop and tell yourself that it is not going to bother you anymore. Instead of worrying about a problem, it makes more sense to look at the solutions to solve that problem. While you can control certain situations, there are some that you have got to ignore and move on.

You may not be able to break all the habits of procrastination in one go. As stated previously, break tasks down and start doing it little by little until you complete everything you need to do. Don't push yourself to do things that you can't do and limit your work time to avoid burnout. Remember to take breaks in between tasks and always remind yourself that you can rather than making yourself feel bad about your work. Don't underestimate yourself, because that is one of the reasons you may start procrastinating again. No matter what, always remind yourself that you will do better, and you will achieve what you want to if you stay focused and positive.

Chapter 5:
Turn Procrastination into Motivation

If you have a lot on your plate and you have not gotten started with your list because you believe you will never manage to get anything done no matter how hard you try, just breathe! There is no denying that people lead hectic lifestyles and they are left with very little time for themselves. While people in the past worked 8-hour shifts, nowadays people spend about 12 to 15 hours to get the job done and this drains them out mentally and physically. If you believe you are not going to finish the job that you have been assigned to do on time, then it's important for you to understand how to positively transform procrastination into motivation and use it to your benefit. Let's be honest, no one likes working overtime, and this can frustrate you and make you feel like you have no time to spend on yourself. If this is something you have been going through, then you need to understand that all you must do is keep yourself motivated and teach yourself how to cut down on the external distractions so you can get work done faster.

Let's start with simple steps and go on to how you can eventually defeat procrastination and motivate yourself to become a better, more positive, and successful person.

The Procrastination Cure (It's Not Eat That Frog!)

Unplug

The first step towards focusing on the task at hand is to unplug and eliminate all unnecessary distractions, specifically your smartphone. Keep your smartphone in a drawer and do not open the drawer until you have finished a certain number of tasks you have assigned to yourself. If you absolutely must check your phone to get in touch with people, use it for no more than two minutes during the quick breaks that you give yourself in between work time. Make it a point not to access unnecessary social media sites or chat applications - if you want to send a message to somebody just dial their number and do it the old-fashioned way for faster communication.

Clean up

It's important for you to avoid distractions and clear the physical clutter around you. If you have a clean workspace you are less likely to get distracted, which is why you should make sure that your workspace is as clean as possible. It's common for people to personalize their work desk and make it look aesthetically pleasing. While an occasional family photograph or your favorite mug is something you can keep on your office desk you may want to limit accessories that are diversions and could distract you. Instead of accessorizing your workspace try keeping motivational quotes around to constantly remind you to get back to work and finish the task at hand.

Write Down Your Distractions

The more you ponder on a distraction, the more irritating it can get, and you will not be able to get your mind off it. If something is distracting you and you are not able to get it out of your head, write it down. When something distracts you and you write it down you will realize that you have managed to eliminate these distractions one at a time more effectively. Apart from thoughts that come into your head, you should also notice the things around you that may distract you. This helps you to limit their usage or get them out of sight so that you can focus more effectively on work. If you have negative reading posters or something that's too violent, distracting or graphic, you may want to get rid of them because these will unknowingly make you feel low and make you start procrastinating because they have a negative impact on your mind. When you surround yourself with positive things you feel positive and are more likely to focus on work, but when there is negativity around you it becomes difficult for you to focus on work.

Read

It important for you to exercise your brain if you want to stop procrastinating because the more active your brain is, the less likely you are to slip into a depressive phase or feel bad about yourself. Reading is the best way to exercise your brain - you may want to do the old-fashioned way or look for a Kindle to read an eBook. The benefits of reading on paper or on a Kindle is that you rest your eyes and get away from technology. There is something about reading an actual book that makes you feel relaxed. It is also great way to fall asleep and ensure that you are properly rested at night.

Take A Walk
If there are too many thoughts going on in your head and you are unable to calm your mind or your nerves before you start working, try going for a walk. Walking helps you to relax and get out all the negative energy - your body will then feel motivated and confident to start working. You don't have to go for a long walk. Even just a 10-minute walk with deep breathing exercises can work wonders to change your mood almost instantly. You can also listen to some soothing music while you are on a walk. This will help you start focusing on positive thoughts and eliminate procrastination and convert it into motivation.

Stay Healthy
You are what you eat, so when you fill junk inside of your body your physiology automatically gets affected. People who eat junk food are more likely to be depressed and sad in comparison to people who eat healthy home-cooked meals regularly. It's important for you to eat healthily and exercise because this helps your mind sharp and gives you the mental energy required to get tasks done. It is also important for you to sleep for a minimum of eight hours every day. If you don't rest well, you won't be able to perform at work well the following day. Sometimes when people procrastinate, they find it difficult to sleep because of the number of negative thoughts that fill up their head. If

you want to rest well and get rid of these thoughts, then you may want to try meditation. If you meditate for a while before you head to bed each day you will manage to sleep more comfortably and be well rested for the following day.

Get Comfortable

If the office environment is too cold or too hot it may affect your productivity. If you notice that you have a lack of focus, then something you can do is to smell a lemon. The scent of a lemon is said to help increase your focus and reduce errors, making you work more effectively. Sitting by your window can also help increase your focus.

Go Green

One of the best ways to increase creativity is to have plants around you, because plants make you feel positive and motivated and they help to improve your focus and concentration. It also makes you feel happy and prevents you from procrastinating.

Use Headphones

If you find it extremely difficult to focus on work then a smart thing for you to do would be to start listening to some soothing music through headphones while working. This helps you increase your concentration and focus a lot better.

When you're in an office environment you can't really use speakers since it will distract the others around you. Speakers don't work well in disconnecting you from the rest of the world and you can still hear external noises when a speaker is on. This doesn't happen when you've got headphones which is why it's preferred.

Meditate
Meditation can help you to relax and get out all the negative thoughts from your mind almost instantly. Meditating for a little while every day not only helps you to concentrate but it also lowers the risk of destructive thoughts. One of the best ways to motivate yourself and convert procrastination into action is to start meditating daily.

Look at Happy Things
Cute pictures and happy photographs are good for you to look at because these make you feel good.

Cut Down on Meetings
Overly frequent meetings can be unnecessary and can take up a large amount of time on planning when you can invest more of that time executing the task. If you are in an authoritative position, make it a point to avoid having too many meetings and try to use that time to do execute tasks. When you do have a meeting, you should make sure the meeting is short and concise so that it is it a productive meeting rather than one that just goes on for no reason.

Delegate Tasks When Possible
While it is important for you to work hard, it also important for you to make rational decisions and think on your feet. If you have talented people who can assist you with a job, make sure that you delegate

some of your responsibilities to them so that the job can be done more effectively and on time. Instead of struggling to get something done, it always is better to have more people help you achieve the goal faster.

Clean Up Your Inbox

The reason it is important for you to clean up your inbox and sort it out is that it saves a lot of time on searching for emails. People these days depend on the internet to get jobs done and the main mode of communication is email which is why your inbox should be as neatly sorted out as possible so that you don't struggle to look for emails or threads. It is just as important for you to have a clean mailbox to work efficiently as it is important for you to have a clear mind.

Track Your Time

Make sure to keep track of how many hours you work during the day and how many breaks you take in between your work time. Doing this on a regular basis will help you to cut down the amount of time that you spend wasted on your break and increase productivity of work. Ideally, try to take no longer than a 10-minute break in an hour and work for at least three hours before you take a longer break. This will contribute in a small but significant way to help you deliver more effective results within the same timeframe.

Automate

We live in a world of technology where you can automate most things to reduce your efforts, and this is something you should take advantage of. Create an RSS feed and have a certain outline ready to be emailed so you don't have to sit and type every email that you must respond to. If you know that you are going to say the same thing to 10 people in a day, it makes sense to have a template ready and only must change a name each time you need to reply. This will save you a couple of minutes for every email you send, and you can put that time to better use.

Similar Tasks

Performing all similar tasks together will help you go from one task to the other more effectively since you are already focused on something that is similar. This will take you lesser time than it would if you had to start the task fresh. At the beginning of each day, make sure you check your task list and identify similar tasks so you can group them together and make the most of the flow you have. This also helps you to finish off these tasks more efficiently.

Limit Typing

It doesn't matter how fast you are typing, it is always faster to speak, which is why you may want to use a speed dictation software to get through most of your work. Instead of writing down most of your things, you can record as much of it as possible to save time.

You're blessed to live in an age where technology is so advanced, make the most of it and use tools that can help you speed up your task, so you get stuff done faster.

Maintain A 'Stop-Doing' List

While it is important for you to have a to-do list to make sure you get through the various things you need to do on a regular basis, it is also important for you to have a 'stop-doing' list which reminds you to eliminate certain things that you would regularly do that eat into your time. This list will continue to remind you of the things that you should avoid - each time you look at it, you will know what commonly distracts you and how you need to avoid that distraction. This is a great way to overcome your procrastination habit and turn it into motivation. While most people tend to focus on a to do list, a 'stop-doing' list is just as important.

Stop Multitasking

It's important for you to understand the priorities of your task and it get done before you move on to the second task. Although a lot of people believe multitasking can help them work better, the truth is that it drains your energy and limits your focus. When you spend time multitasking, not only do you end up not being able to be efficient in one task, but you also confuse yourself and never manage to pay full attention to a task.

Try the Must, Should, Want Method

This method helps you to identify important tasks and your immediate and long-term goals that you need to complete. This is something that you should do daily and work towards achieving all three goals by prioritizing them based on importance. The must-do tasks are the ones that are most important, should-do tasks are ones you need to focus on, and the wants are the tasks that help you get closer to your long-term goals but that you should focus on last.

Avoid Checking Emails on Your Commute

Checking emails is a high priority task but this isn't something you should be doing on your commute because you invest double the amount of time checking your emails when you reach work. You end up double checking them again when you want to reply. Instead, give yourself enough time to go to your inbox when you are settled down at work so you can reply to them the same time you read them, saving on the time you invested initially opening and reading through each mail. This also lowers the risk of losing an important mail or missing out on one because you forgot to mark it unread it after checking it.

Do That "One Thing"

Ask yourself what is most important and make sure that you get that one thing done effectively. Try to ask yourself every day about the one thing that you want to get done during that day and make sure that you do it first.

Choose Your Important Task Wisely

Look at the list of tasks that you have and pick the most important first, so you get it done at a time when you are most energetic and when you are most focused. You can choose to write the tasks on a sheet of paper and stick it to your computer screen or somewhere where you can look at it over and over again, so you keep reminding yourself that this task is pending. It's important for you to remind yourself because not only does this motivate you to work a little harder but it ensures that you don't forget about it.

Start with Creative Work

It is important for you to focus on creative tasks and get them finished first because that's when your brain is fresh, and you can think better. Always try to finish tasks that require your mind to focus more effectively faster than leave it for the second half of the day when you are mentally drained out. Your creative tasks turn out to be better when they are done with a fresh mind and you also end up in investing leisure time doing it.

Be Picky

It's essential for you to be picky about the kind of work you choose because if you end up doing almost anything and everything that comes your way, you burden yourself with too much work and you will not be able to handle it as effectively as you would like to. While it is important to stay busy and have a full work day it's not recommended to bite off more than you can chew because this will affect the overall quality of your work. If you have a clear mindset, you will end up choosing the kind of work you want to accept and pick the things that you know you will be able to complete effectively and confidently. Instead of comparing how much money a task will make, try to ask you yourself how effectively you will be able to complete these tasks.

Plan Your To-Do List the Night Before

It is very important to have a to-do list on a regular basis. The best way to make the most out of your to-do list is to plan the night before. You will have a clear idea of what your following day looks like and how well you will be able to handle the tasks that you have planned for the day. This habit saves you time of having to sit down and make a to do list at the start of your day and enables you to put that time into doing something more fruitful.

Always Sort Tasks Based on Priority

It's important for you to sort out your tasks based on priority, focusing on ones that are most important and moving on to the ones that are less important by the end of the day. When you start your day, you are always more motivated, and you will be able to put all your energy into doing important and urgent tasks better. If something goes wrong during the day and you are not able to complete the remainder of your tasks you know for sure that you managed to finish the important ones and you only missed out on the ones that were not so important or not so urgent.

Always Ask Yourself Five Questions:

- Does the solution help you get closer to your goal?

- Is it important to your employer/your boss?

- Does it help you earn good money?

- Does it make your life easier?

- Do you need to complete it urgently?

When you have the answer to these questions not only will you be able to prioritize effectively but you will manage to eliminate the tasks that are not so important, and it will help plan your day to deliver better results.

Break Down Your Tasks into Subtasks

As we had discussed before, you need to break down your tasks into smaller portions so that you are able to deal with them effectively. When breaking down the tasks try to focus on creating sub-tasks that are no longer than 30 minutes each because this will allow you to put in more effort into completing the task and you'll also stay focused and achieve better results. When you break your tasks into 30-minute sub tasks, you end up doing them more effectively.

The Two-Minute Rule

If there are small tasks on your plate that will require less than 2 minutes to complete, give yourself a certain amount of time to finish as many of those tasks as possible. This will help you to increase your motivation, and in case you are having a bad day, or you are not available you would have still managed to get quite a lot of your tasks done by simply focusing on the smaller ones.

Eat the Frog

The big tasks are usually the ones you dread most, so focus on breaking it down into small pieces try to complete as much of the tasks as possible when you are still fresh. This will help you overcome procrastination and motivate yourself. It's always recommended to start off with the tougher tasks so you can get done with it early in the day. If you can't manage to look at a tough task, break it down!

When you look at a big task, you tend to feel less motivated to begin working on it, but the minute you break it down into smaller ones you get going and manage to complete it in a short time span. This helps you increase productivity without stressing about big tasks and increases efficiency.

Find Your Biological Prime Time

Everyone has a "prime time" - a magical time where you are most motivated, or you can get a maximum amount of work done. When you are in this zone, you try to put in as much energy as you can to do work because it's the time when you will be good at what you do, and your productivity will be at its peak.

Visible Progress

It's important for you to be able to monitor and measure your progress because this will help you figure out how well you are doing, and it continues to motivate you to push harder. If you don't see results, it's difficult for you to continue your work and this will push you back instead of motivating you to move forward.

Don't Break the Chain

Make it a point to set goals for yourself every day and continue finding your rhythm without breaking the chain. There are going to be external factors from time to time that may affect the way you think or make you feel a little low, but your focus should be to remember to stick to your plan.

Start Challenging Yourself

Time yourself every week and see how long it takes you to complete a task. Start challenging yourself to complete them in shorter time spans but in realistic time frames. Give yourself a small reward every time you achieve something - treating yourself when you achieve a goal makes you feel good and this helps to enhance your productivity. It's important to stay in a good mood and constantly motivate yourself towards getting better. When you have a positive attitude, you've already won half the battle!

Stay Confident

No matter what kind of job you have it is important for you to do it with confidence and believe in yourself. When you stop telling yourself that you are good at what you do, and you'll be able to complete your work effectively not only will you get better results, but you will feel motivated to do the work. Always keep a strong posture with your chin up because at the end of the day your posture matters and your confidence will increase.

Be Happy

The most important way you will be able to increase your productivity is when you are happy. Do little things every day to put a smile on your face because this not only makes you feel better, but it eliminates procrastination and diverts your mind towards motivation.

These little changes may not seem like a lot but when you incorporate them and begin enjoying your life, not only will you benefit from them, but you'll also manage to successfully transform your procrastination into motivating yourself to do better each day.

Chapter 6:
Time Management Strategies by Millionaires

It's no secret that millionaires have made choices which have led them on the path of success. Therefore, they become role models for almost everyone. If you want to think like a millionaire, it's important for you to use their time and management secrets so you learn how to balance your day more effectively and understand what choices need to be made and how to make the right decisions when it matters most. There is no denying that a millionaire has a better sense of time management as compared to other people and they understand exactly what to do with the time and how to use it most effectively. Considering they need to deal with at least a thousand emails a day, they also need to figure out how they are going to communicate effectively with their employees and schedule meetings to organize strategies for their work. Successful people simply make the right decisions because it is necessary to make informed decisions to help the team get on the path of success. Here are some interesting facts about millionaires that you should keep in mind:

Most millionaires wake up early in the morning because they like to spend time with their families. They understand how important it is to maintain a work/life balance and they do what it takes to make the most of the time they have. This includes waking up early to prepare breakfast for their kids just to see them smile!

They always find time to exercise because fitness is important and with a healthy body comes a healthy mind, which helps them to focus on work better. While some people always find an excuse to not exercise, a millionaire is usually looking for ways to fit in a workout even if it's just for 15 minutes. They like working out regularly because it gives them more energy and helps them to cope with tough days and balance out energy when they need it.

They pay a lot of attention to reading because it helps them to learn more information and it helps to exercise the brain regularly. Apart from physical exercise, millionaires also make it a point to read regularly so they can exercise their brain and learn new things. Even after they have accomplished most of what they had set out to do, they continue challenging themselves every day!

Eliminate Time Spent in Meetings

Several businesses often believe that investing unnecessary time in a meeting is not going to benefit them. You need to figure out what's important and what isn't for your business so you can profit from it more effectively. Instead of wasting time talking to your employees regarding what needs to be done, it makes more sense to just let them do the work. When less time is spent in meetings you can spend more time getting the job done rather than discussing how it needs to be done. Take note of tasks that you believe are unnecessary and eliminate them from the workspace completely. Use automated tools and shared drives that make it easier for your employees to coordinate with one another so that can you get more effective results out of them and so they end up working at higher efficiency levels.

If you absolutely must have a meeting with your employees, have a meeting that is no longer than 10 minutes. Make sure to cover up everything you want to convey in the meeting in clear communication and then get that employee to communicate to others. Meetings don't need to be long. So, don't let a meeting last too long where employees will end up getting demotivated. Have a quick meeting discussing important aspects of the work and carry on getting the job done.

Start Your Day with A Bang

It is important for you to use your energy to complete tasks that matter, and this is exactly what all millionaires do as well. While people have a misconception that they should have meetings at the start of the day, the truth is, meetings are not a priority and they can be left for the end of the day just before the employees leave so that people know what they need to do starting the following day. The more important the task, the better it is to get it done in the earlier part of your day because you have a lower chance of distraction and distractions are also fewer in comparison to when you have an office full of people constantly asking you to do things.

Have Themed Days

It's important for you to raise the motivation levels of your employees so you should always plan different kinds of themes from time to time in the organization. It can be difficult if you must work too many hours a day, but if you learn how to delegate your work effectively you will be able to be more productive and get more out of your employees than expected. Themed days help to keep your employees in control and makes them very disciplined which is essential to accomplish success. It takes over distractions and it ensures that the employees understand the importance of getting the job done on time. Some theme examples include:

- Mondays for management
- Tuesdays for product
- Wednesdays for marketing
- Thursdays for partnership
- Fridays for culture
- Saturdays for holiday
- Sundays for reflection and preparation for Monday

Discipline Is Essential

It's very important to keep motivation levels high in your organization but you also need to maintain a certain level of discipline if you want your employees to be productive. Hiring a team of intelligent employees aren't going to benefit you if they are not productive. The only way they will be able to be productive is when they have discipline and they follow the rules. When you have a team of people not only look for smart ones but look for the ones who are disciplined because this will manage to improve your business. The kind of employees you hire at the end of the day will help to build your business or destroy it completely.

Recharge and Refresh Midday
If you are going to continue working for long periods of time, don't do that without a break as it's not going to benefit you. You should yourself a break in between so that you can continue to work at the same pace you started off with during the day. This is one of the main reasons why it's important to break down the tasks at hand and give yourself breaks in between so that you manage to do it effectively rather than stress about completing the whole thing in one go. Millionaires tend to take shorter breaks during the day, so they keep motivation levels high and have the same amount of energy that they did at the start of the day right until the end. This helps them to deliver quality work from start to finish. The little breaks you take will benefit you in the long run because you never feel overwhelmed.

Focus on Creating Good Product Rather Than Making Money

The Procrastination Cure (It's Not Eat That Frog!)

If you want to stay in business long-term you must provide quality services and products because that's what will help you make money automatically. Your main motive shouldn't be to make money but rather to create products that will satisfy customers and will be available to them at an affordable price. Continue to think about innovative products and interesting ways you will be able to better your product every day.

Let this be your motivation to move forward and let it encourage you to do something that you know is good. This helps to foster a feel-good factor which automatically increases the amount of work you do and the quality of the work too. Remember, when you are a business owner you create job opportunities and there are a lot of people who depend on your business. Not only should you focus on growing your business for your benefit but also for the benefit of the employees who work under your wing. When you consider their success as yours not only does your business grow more effectively but it also makes you feel good and that motivates you to get to work every day and do better.

Learn to Give Yourself More Time

When you are in the middle of a busy work schedule, the one thing that you need to remember is to give yourself enough me time so that you can relax and resume work again before you are burdened with more tasks to do. During your 'do not disturb' time, all you need to do is relax and let go of all the planning in your head so that you can

Stephen N. Murphy

prepare yourself for the following tasks. No matter how busy you are, you should always find time to relax during a tough day at work because this helps you to focus better and realize what you could do better. If you constantly bury yourself in work without giving yourself a break, you will experience burn out.

Chapter 7:
The Secret to Building Self-Discipline

In order for you to overcome procrastination, you need to have strong self-discipline, so you don't allow yourself to get tempted every step you take. While you don't expect yourself to improve yourself instantly, it's a learning process and every step you take can help you get closer to your desired goal. There are many things that you can do in order to build your self-discipline and stay strong but here are some effective secrets that are known to work.

Know Your Weaknesses

The first stage of getting self-discipline in place is to recognize your weaknesses and accept that you have some. Everyone wants to believe that they are strong, and they don't have any weakness, but the truth is that there are many things that could be a weakness for you and in order to get better you got to overcome weaknesses effectively and turn it into your strengths.

The first step is to confront the weaknesses you have so that you can identify them effectively and understand exactly how to deal with it.

There are solutions for every weakness, and they can easily be converted into strengths with a little effort. This is something you must continuously remind yourself about because if you don't acknowledge your weakness you will never be able to deal with it in the first place.

If you don't manage to recognize your weaknesses on your own, you can always consult people you trust and ask them to help you out. You need to be prepared to face a few critiques you may not like but that is part of the process of learning and becoming self-disciplined. Once you identify your weakness it is easier for you to learn how to withstand it and fight it in a more streamlined manner.

Your weakness doesn't necessarily have to be a distraction or a flaw that you give into, it could also be something at work or a task you may not be good at.

You need to prepare yourself to hear the truth about the various kinds of tasks that you can and can't you do so that you know how to deal with them and you do not waste time on attempting something you may not manage to get done as effectively as you would like to.

If your weakness lies at work and there is a portion of a task you can't get done and it haunts you every time you get to it, give it to somebody who may be good at it.

When you ask somebody to get the work that you are not good at done, you maintain consistency in your work, and you know for a fact that you will be able to get it completed on time without procrastination in the process. When you come across something you are weak at, there is a chance that you give into temptation and deviate from the task at hand. This could cause you to end up losing focus but when you hand it over to somebody else you can continue working at a steady pace without reaching a breaking point during your work schedule. You also need to remember not to stress about perfection because that's one of the major problems of procrastinating and if you want everything to be perfect you will never manage to finish a task on time.

Attempt to try different ways to solve the problem. A wise entrepreneur once said that aggregation is the mother of invention, so if you don't have the skills try again with a different approach. Try to learn how others manage to deal with it and see if you can get some insights on converting that weakness of yours into a strength.

Remove Temptations

Temptations are something that waste your time and make you procrastinate because people end up postponing a job that needs to be done so they can indulge in a temptation. While some people have more control over temptation than others, giving in to temptation at the wrong time will often make some of the temptations turn into obsessions and when this happens, your productivity decreases drastically. Due to this you won't be able to figure out how you can self-discipline yourself again. If you want to make sure you don't give in to temptation you need to learn how to deal with it tactfully and learn how to say no at the right times.

The first stage is to identify a potential temptation and learn how to control the temptation, not just temporarily, but permanently and for the long-term. Whether it is the urge to get up from your work desk and go smoke or whether it is to delay an important project, you need to learn what interferes with your long-term goal and how you can stay focused. Binge eating and smoking is bad for health and it will make you feel low and guilty after you have given into the temptation. If your temptations are high, you may want to ask people to help you to control it. If you are a smoker and you do not want to smoke in between your project, then try to keep your pack of cigarettes away from you and promise yourself not to touch it until you have finished your task at hand. Similarly, if you are craving to binge eat then you can replace your unhealthy option with a healthy snack so that you don't feel bad about snacking. The kind of food you eat can help increase or decrease your productivity so make your choices wisely.

Learn to remove yourself from temptation in the long run. If you crave to smoke a cigarette and you are trying to quit, make sure that you get rid of anything and everything that reminds you of smoking, so it gets easier for you not to give in to the temptation. You must remember that temptation takes a while to get over completely so don't force yourself into a situation where it affects your productivity but rather try to control it little by little until you achieve your desired goal. Remember, when there is something that tempts you, try to tell yourself that there is also a solution to the problem that may be better for you rather than giving in to the temptation because this will help to self-discipline yourself more effectively.

Be honest with yourself because if you keep lying to yourself and giving into temptation, it won't help you progress. One of the first things you need to do is be honest because if you cheat and lie to people about not giving into temptation when you do, you will start feeling guilty and this will affect your productivity more than you would have expected.

If your urge to give in to a temptation increases drastically, imagine yourself resisting it in your head. A visual interpretation of rejecting something can make you stronger and believe that you can achieve it. You need to work towards building a strong resistance against temptation if you want to handle it effectively.

Whenever you have the urge to give in to a temptation, try to think about the consequences the temptation will eventually lead to. Whether it is wasting time instead of focusing on work, giving in to the urge of smoking, or even binging on unhealthy food it's not going to do you any good, so you need to realize that the sooner you learn how to resist this temptation, the more fruitful and successful your life will become. Remind yourself of all the bad things the temptations can eventually lead to and this will help you to stay strong. If the temptation becomes really bad, then you may want to try distracting yourself for a bit so that the temptation passes by. Sometimes simply closing your eyes and meditating for a few minutes can help you overcome the strongest of temptations and make you feel good about yourself and get you back on track at work. This technique works well with smokers who constantly crave smoking and are trying to give up. When you are faced with temptation but overcome those first few minutes, you'll be able to resist and be strong on your path of self-discipline.

You need to have a mindset that tells you firmly you will not give in no matter what and that this is a stepping stone towards becoming more self-disciplined in life.

Set Clear Goals and Have an Execution Plan

One of the best ways to become more self-disciplined is to set goals for yourself. These goals don't necessarily need to revolve around your work and they can be anything from something as simple as making sure that you get up at a particular time every day and head to bed at a particular time, or more challenging, for example, eating healthy food at least five days a week and exercising for a few minutes every day. When you plan your goals, you need to plan them in a realistic manner so that you don't slip and fall back into old habits because you are too hard on yourself. Avoid setting goals that are too difficult to achieve as you may end up disappointing yourself and losing interest in the goal completely.

The Procrastination Cure (It's Not Eat That Frog!)

While you should always aim very high you need to start low and keep celebrating in between so that you're motivated to go on. There are different ways to set goals for yourself - if you want to set a goal to help you focus better at work you can create a chart that tells you what must be done at each hour of the day and aim towards achieving it. If you want to overcome your temptations, then setting goals is a great way to do this because it helps you to become more self-disciplined and you'll train your mind to do the right thing.

For a lot of people their cell phones are a huge distraction during the day and one of the best ways to deal with this is to set a goal of not touching your phone at hours unless you need to make an important phone call.

Scrolling through your social media platforms and seeing what others are up to is not going to get you anywhere, so you need to train your mind to stay off social media platforms when you are focusing and work more efficiently. That's a goal you should aim to achieve every day. Give yourself short breaks in between your work schedule and allow yourself to indulge in your social media addiction for a few minutes during that break. If you fail to keep up to your goal and you still go and check these applications on your phone in between your work schedule, penalize yourself by not doing it for the rest of the day. When you start training yourself to focus and be more productive not only do you incorporate self-discipline, but you also become more effective in what you do. You will realize that by eliminating small temptations not only do you end up performing better but you get more time for yourself that you can utilize to do more productive work. If you want to be successful you need to put the maximum time into working and focus at achieving your goals both in the long-term and short-term on a regular basis. While long-term goals are essential, it is also important for you to have short-term goals because these can eventually lead you to your long-term goal. Just like with a big task that you break down into multiple smaller tasks to make it easier, you need to do the same with your goals so that you can achieve it a little at a time.

Many times, people ask other people to help set goals for them. This is something you should avoid completely because when another person sets the goal for you, you don't feel as motivated towards working on the goal as you would when you set one yourself. They also don't know your limits which means you can either end up with a goal that is too simple to achieve or one that's extremely difficult.

You also need to be clear about what your success looks like so that you can aim high and working hard towards achieving it. Always have a plan in place so you don't go astray, and you learn how to self-discipline yourself one step at a time. You get to value the importance of your goals because your goal is your end target, and this is what will keep you motivated towards doing better and understanding the importance of self-discipline in your life.

Focus your eyes on the prize; this is something that will keep you positive even on the lowest of days. If you want to achieve your goal on time you have to track your performance to make sure you don't slip away from the final target and that you work hard every day towards achieving it.

Build Your Self-Discipline

Self-discipline isn't something that you were born with. For you to become a self-disciplined person you need to work hard. There are various things that you can do in order to achieve self-discipline but teaching it to yourself one step at a time works in your favor. Make sure you understand what your goal is before you start self-disciplining yourself because self-discipline works on the principle of controlling a certain situation. You need to identify what that situation is for you to discipline yourself. Find out the reasons why because it's important for you to know them. A good reason for self-discipline is that it is the fuel that helps you pump in more energy into focusing and inspiring yourself every day of your life. Keep asking yourself what you want to do, how you want to do it, and why you want to do it, and once you have gotten the answers for this, constantly remind yourself that these are the reasons you want to teach yourself self-discipline. Self-discipline does require a lot of commitment and accountability which means it is likely you may be diverted into thoughts that are unnecessary. You must hold yourself accountable for every action you make, so make sure you understand why you have done it so that you are able to control the situation.

If you want to instill this in yourself, you need to remind yourself that you cannot blame others for the choices you make and that no matter what situation you are in it's important to identify how you are going to deal with it in an effective manner. While it is good to reward yourself for something that you have done well, it is also needed that you penalize yourself when you do something wrong. When you correct yourself for a mistake you committed or a slip up you had, it helps you to not repeat the same mistake again and encourages you to do better. Everyone has temptations but learning to deal with them in an effective way is what self-discipline is all about. The sooner you understand what you need to do versus what you want to do and figure out which is more important, you will be able to master the skill of self-discipline.

You hold yourself accountable for your self-discipline skills so it's up to you to decide what level of self-discipline you want to set for yourself. You can choose to be extremely hard on yourself or give yourself a little leverage depending on your goal and the number of temptations or distractions you have in life. You need to ask yourself various questions and determine where you stand before you decide the standard of self-discipline you want to incorporate in your life. Forcing yourself to lead a very reclusive life when you are a social person may be difficult and something that is unrealistic for you to achieve.

It would be better for you to aim at choosing a simple yet effective technique that allows you to indulge in a little temptation every now and then so you can get back to focusing on your tasks.

Create New Habits

There are various things that you can do in order to focus on self-discipline but the most important is to create a habit that you can work with and use it to your benefit.

It's important for you to know that you can be motivated with what is important to you. You need to understand that your goal is not to watch the motivation happen but rather the commitment towards the task and getting it done on time which is why you need commitment rather than motivation. One of the most important things for you is to be committed long-term towards getting your job done regularly without the distractions of any other temptations. You should be disciplined and continue working even on days where you don't feel motivated.

You also need to understand that when you get a job done you should not just look at the results but rather how much you know about the task so that you can deliver quality of work. It's very important for you to focus on being positive because without good quality you will never be able to deliver the results that you want. As I stated above, if you find it difficult to get a certain portion of your task completed because you lack the skills, you need to work towards building on that skill rather than getting frustrated.

Make it an exciting and fun journey when you work because this will make you work more effectively, and it will help you enjoy what you do every day of your life. The one thing you should remember is to always be happy with the task you have in hand because it will make you feel satisfied. You need to try and get rid of negative feelings because these negative feelings will hold you back and it will leave you stagnant in a profession. When you teach yourself self-discipline, the one thing that you need to remember is to encourage yourself to do better and not stagnate in one place for very long. If you want to achieve success, you must constantly move ahead and make better choices in life to improve on the life you live. This will happen if you are happy with the kind of work you do. You can learn to enjoy your work in an effective way so that you spend most of your time doing it rather than procrastinating. You should also use your imagination and focus on the positive attributes of life that make you feel happy instead of thinking negative thoughts that will pull down your energy. If you want to challenge yourself, you should do it because this will force you to do something and when you do it with a smile on your face you will enjoy everything you do towards getting closer to success.

Not only will you manage to become better at self-discipline, but you will also get better at the kind of work you deliver, bringing you closer towards success. When you want to motivate yourself every now and then you should push yourself when necessary. If you really want to do something you need to challenge yourself and commit to learning how to get it done the right way. If you have been given a task, break it up into parts and see if you can get it done on your own. If you can't delegate, then try to figure out the way to learn this task one bit at a time because then you no longer must depend on someone to get your job done.

The more you challenge yourself, the better you will get because you start teaching yourself by practicing more and this works out in your favor in the long run.

You might be wondering if your current path will make you successful or not. Using motivational words or phrases multiple times a day will make you believe in your ability. You also need to watch what you eat because the truth is, the kind of food you eat helps you to either increase your productivity and this also determines how successful you will be eventually.

There are several food items that help you feel positive while there are some that can make you feel low and negative and increase procrastination. If you want to be successful, not only do you need to self-discipline yourself but also change the kind of food that you eat. Eating junk food is something that will ruin your system and will encourage medical problems such as hormonal imbalance and thyroid issues that make you slower and more lethargic, thereby limiting your ability to work to your full potential. Similarly, when you eat healthy meals at regular intervals your energy levels are always high, and you will be able to get the job done without any distractions.

One of the best ways to eat healthy is to eat home-cooked meals that are not prepared using too much oil and give you a complete balanced diet which includes green vegetables as well as your required protein. It may surprise you that the color of fruit also has a huge impact on your life and fruits that are fresh and come in different colors, especially the bright ones, will make you feel happy and lift your spirits. One of the best ways to stay successful is to start eating healthy and fresh meals because fresh food manages to make you feel fit almost instantly.

While several people depend on caffeine to keep their energy levels high and help them to focus through a tough day at work, this might not be a good solution for you as it interferes with your ability to think. It is also known to cause sleep deprivation, so if you have a cup of coffee a little later in the day you may struggle to fall asleep. This will affect your following day and make you feel tired and drowsy and this will hamper your ability to work effectively. Self-discipline is important because it will help you plan to eat regularly and when you eat your meals on time you will provide your body with the proper nutrients that make you healthier. If you want to be successful you need to look after your health, and it all begins with what you eat.

The Procrastination Cure (It's Not Eat That Frog!)

If you're eating habits are bad and you end up eating at wrong times of the day, the smart thing for you to do would be to stock up on healthy snacks including fruits that you can eat even while you are working. Not only does this help keep your energy levels up but it also helps you feel full and happy. When you remain hungry, the irritability begins, and you will not be able to stay as focused on your job as you would with a full stomach.

When looking to follow a healthy diet you should remember that moderation is very important and if you start to eat too much of one thing it is not going to benefit you in any way. Focusing only on eating salads will not give you the amount of energy you need to go through the day which means you have to get your fair share of protein as well. Take your time to craft out a diet plan that gives you all the essential nutrients you need in order to keep you energized. Some people also choose to take a multivitamin at the start of the day - while it is not necessary, you could pick one up at a local drug store. While some people are against the thought of using a multivitamin, it is good for you because it provides the body with all the necessary nutrients that you need.

How you eat also matters because some people don't really care about where they sit while eating or how fast they end up eating their food. Some people turn on the television and start eating larger meals because they want to go through the entire television series or program that they started watching while eating. If the program is soon going to end, they end up chewing their food a lot faster and this does not foster healthy digestion. If you want your digestive system to work properly you must chew your food well so that you digest it and boost your metabolism levels. High metabolism levels mean more energy and the ability to get more done during the day.

It is important for you to work at your full potential and eating a healthy meal is one of the habits you may have to get used to before you adapt to it completely.

Change Your Perception About Willpower

If you want to accomplish something, it is important for you to set the right habits and make self-discipline a part of your regular routine so that you don't have to prepare yourself every day to stay focused and get the job done correctly. This is not going to happen immediately, and it would require a lot of willpower for you to make this possible. The habits that you have are usually formed because of a routine that you were used to following and it's not going to break the minute you decide you no longer benefit from a habit. Unfortunately, losing the bad habit may be more difficult than changing good habits so you must make sure that you figure out how you will start changing to get habituated to the right things.

When you build good habits, it helps you to conserve a lot of resources and put them to use effectively and this helps you to save energy when needed the most. It helps you to relax in stressful situations and overcome anxiety problems so that you don't worry about whether you will be able to get through the day or not.

Habits are formed in the brain, which means getting rid of a habit is difficult and instead of training yourself to overcome a habit you need to start training yourself to introducing habits that work well for you. Give yourself time to train your brain to develop healthy habits that incorporate self-discipline in your life, and this will benefit you in the long run. Rome wasn't built in a day and good habits won't come to you instantly either. It's a struggle and you must give up a lot of old habits and form new ones that help you to stay strong and increase willpower. The best way to overcome bad habits is to learn to say no and not give into temptation little by little. No matter what you are dealing with, always try to approach the situation one step at a time because it makes the journey that much easier.

When you are planning to set a good habit or a good example for yourself, you need to remember that you can't just stray from the actual goal because this is what matters most. You need to have a healthy routine to follow but not make it something you will be paranoid about or must put all your energy into. It's a small change you need to make on a regular basis, so you get used to it and become part of your routine life. This helps to incorporate self-discipline long-term and more effectively.

Give Yourself A Backup Plan

Backup plans are smaller agreements that you can keep going back to and altering to suit your preference. A lot of people believe that it's important to have a backup plan in order to become successful so that if you fail at plan A, you can immediately switch to plan B. This may seem really efficient and low-risk which is why it's so popular, but the truth is having a plan can not only increase the chances of procrastination, but it also diverts your mind from self-discipline because you always know you have a plan B to depend on.

If you want to be successful, the number one thing you need to do is keep yourself off the leverage of being able to switch to another plan and believe that this is your only option. People who usually switch to plan B tend to mess up the second plan as well because they won't able to focus on it and get it done the first time and chances that they will mess it up again are quite high.

When you have a plan B you tend to take plan A lightly, and this does not work well for your success rate which is why you must think about your initial plan as the only option to work with if you want to succeed. The reason you choose plan A to begin with is because you believe it's the right way to go about a situation, so don't second doubt yourself.

Forgive Yourself and Move Forward

We are all human, and this means that there will be times when we end up making mistakes. Sometimes these mistakes are a little more severe than we would imagine, and this often leads us to get upset about the situation. Things may not always work out the way you planned, and while it's not good to have a plan B, you need to start fresh instead of not being able to move on. Forgiveness is important for you to move on and without forgiving yourself you will not be able to take the next step ahead. There are various stages to forgiveness and if you want to start anew then you must go through all the stages so that you do not repeat the same mistake. The first stage of forgiveness begins with responsibility. You need to take responsibility for the wrong that you have done so you can work your way up the ladder towards the other stages. Sometimes people procrastinate at the first stage and they refuse to accept that they have made a mistake. Once you admit that you are at fault, you then need to work towards the second stage which is remorse.

You need to feel remorse for the situation you put yourself in and all your coworkers or friends for that matter and feel bad about it. Unless you feel bad about a mistake you made, you will not be able to correct it so you need to bring yourself to this stage and by taking responsibility before you are ready to move to the third stage. The third stage of forgiveness is restoration. This is where you begin to plan your tasks all over again and do it with confidence so that you will not fail. Once you are on this stage you can then begin executing your plan and go towards the final stage of renewal. It's important for you to understand and forgive yourself for the mistakes you have made and moving on without holding any guilt or bad taste regarding the experience. Self-discipline is also about controlling the way you feel about your emotions. If you want to be successful and you want to make the most out of your life you must learn to get ahold of your emotions, so you are able to deal with the most complex situations with finesse.

Chapter 8:
Essential Phrases to Stop Procrastinating

There are six P's that you need to keep in mind that will help you avoid procrastination: Prior Planning Prevents Piss Poor Performance. These 6 Ps are the key to ensuring that you plan well in advance and take care of performance issues.

Prior Planning Prevents Piss Poor Performance

These are the 6 P's that you need to keep in mind when you want to avoid procrastination. Planning is the key element to making sure that you get tasks completed on time. If you want to make sure that you are finishing a task within a given time frame, then you need to start planning well in advance. When you are given a task at work and you need to complete that within the next couple of days, it makes more sense to start taking care of the task the very same day that you receive it. Putting it on the back burner and waiting until the very last day will not help you deliver quality performance. Often, procrastination leads to extremely poor performance and this is what the 6 P's will tell you. When you plan and strategize well in advance you will eliminate the possibility of poor performance.

Physically Preparing for Things

There are several things that you may be mentally prepared to do, however, when the time comes to go ahead and do it, it becomes difficult. One classic example is planning to go to the gym. Everyone has done this at least once in their lifetime. You end up spending money on an expensive gym membership and you do not have the motivation to head to the gym. This is where physical preparation will help you. If you know that you must head to the gym at 6:00 in the morning, then you should try and sleep in your gym clothes. As silly as this may sound, it is actually a very helpful exercise because when you wake up you will already be physically prepared to go to the gym and there will be no excuse left for you. If you decide not to go to the gym, then you will have to change and get into your home clothes. The task of having to change early in the morning can deter you from changing and it will motivate you to head to the gym. When you physically prepare, it makes it very easy for you to go ahead and complete your task.

Try and Visualize Your Problems

When you start visualizing your problems you will start fearing the consequences and this will push you towards completing your task. Have you ever noticed that you are anxious to complete your tasks on time when there is a fear of your boss standing over you? These are the kind of consequences that you need to visualize, and this will help you face your problems and complete tasks without having to procrastinate.

Plan for Tomorrow

When you start your day, you need to make sure that you plan. When you do not have a plan in place, your brain will not know which direction to head towards and this will leave you wandering without any purpose for the day. You need to make sure that you plan everything well in advance and this will help your brain plans various activities. This can be seen in the example of studying for an exam. If you know that you have a science exam the next day, you should create a plan that will help you cover certain topics as soon as you wake up. This will help your brain to be mentally prepared and you will be able to prepare well for the exam.

Chapter 9:
The 5-Second Rule Mind Hack

When it comes to working towards success and doing things that can help you improve your lifestyle and get closer to your goals, the 5-second rule comes in handy. There are a lot of reasons why this rule works, and one of them is that it's not time-consuming. As the name suggests, it is a 5-second rule and it needs to be acted upon within 5 seconds of the conception of the idea so that your brain doesn't shun the idea completely. This concept was designed by Mel Robbins, and according to Mel, if you have an intuitive desire to work on a goal or accomplish something you need to physically move and initiate action by the end of the fifth second without wasting any more time. All you have is a 5-second window where you have an extremely high motivation level and you will be able to make the decision right there and then without any change of plans.

With the 5-second rule, you need to remember that there are five elements in it and each element is equally important. The process begins with you counting backwards from 5 to 1. This begins with the first second, and this is the moment when you have an instinct. When we talk about an instinct, it needs to be a healthy, positive one and not

The Procrastination Cure (It's Not Eat That Frog!)

something that will affect your mindset or your lifestyle negatively. If you have the urge to go buy an expensive cell phone, that is not a positive instinct. However, if you suddenly realize that there is an interesting topic you want to start writing about because you believe it's going to be a bestseller you need to start working on it within 5-seconds so that the bubbles of wisdom inside of you start creating an ocean of knowledge that you can start flowing out of your system. The minute you have an impulse or an instinct to do something you need to act upon it almost instantly, and this is where the second element comes in. The second element is to act on the goal; this is crucial because you need to make sure this is a choice of getting up and walking towards doing what you believe is really going to be effective in your life. If you decide that you want to write a book and you already selected the topic then the second goal is achieved. We often refer to the 5-second rule as a gut feeling and a feeling that we often ignore believing it's just a passing phase. What we don't realize is this feeling can sometimes help you succeed more effectively than any other plans ever will.

After you decide you want to go ahead with the goal, you come to the third element - this is to push yourself to go ahead and act. Once you have decided and as soon as you know that it's right, you must push yourself, establish from ground level, and build on the idea of writing your book. This is where you take control of the situation and decide what needs to be done for you to move ahead with this decision of yours. You just need to picture what you believe you want to do and then move on to the next element which is to move within the next 5 seconds.

This may seem very complicated to you and you may be wondering how you can accomplish all of this within 5 seconds. You don't have to! Every element in Mel Robbins' book requires 5 seconds for you to decide and that's the reason it is called the 5-second rule. From the minute the idea was conceived in your brain you need to give yourself 5 seconds to feel in your heart that your decision is the right decision and you are not going to fail when you go ahead with the plan. If you get a positive feeling about the idea it is something worth moving on with and you go to your final element which is to act, or your brain will forget about it. This is where you either pick up the phone and let somebody know what you are doing or note it down on a piece of paper so that you remind yourself that you plan to do this. If somebody comes up with multiple of these ideas in a day but the 5-second window destroys the ideas, those ideas aren't fruitful and not important. Subconsciously we have multiple such ideas throughout the day but only a few sticks out and these are the ones you need to look out for.

If you want the 5-second rule to prove beneficial to you, it is important for you to start living a lifestyle that is healthy and to self-discipline yourself. It's not easy to think positive thoughts when you have a negative mindset - a negative and emotional person will not be able to work towards the path of success confidently. Procrastination

The Procrastination Cure (It's Not Eat That Frog!)

is one of the leading causes of failure and if you want to become successful you need to take your first step towards overcoming procrastination and making yourself a stronger and more successful person one step at a time. This is not a difficult choice to make. It is something you can do very effectively when you put your mind to it. Whether it is changing your bad habits or incorporating the 5-second rule, the minute you learn how to challenge yourself you will start to see change and this change would be for the better.

Chapter 10:
The Japanese Technique to Overcome Laziness

Almost everyone has had a goal in their life only to realize that they were heading towards failure after a few weeks or months. If you want to challenge yourself and overcome laziness then it's important for you to accept that although you are not ready, you need to push yourself to do it now and not tomorrow or next week. While you always start off something with a lot of motivation it will eventually end up fading out and we lose interest in the goal that we planned to set out to achieve. One of the major reasons this happens is because we try to achieve too much too fast and the new responsibilities that we have taken up don't work well to help us change our old habits and adjust to the new ones.

One of the reasons why it's important for you to understand how essential it is to incorporate change one step at a time is because this helps you to achieve success and no matter how long it takes to you to train your body, it is always going to be worth it. If you want to overcome procrastination, then the Japanese technique for overcoming laziness is something you may want to try out. This method is known as Kaizen, also referred to as the one-minute principle.

The Procrastination Cure (It's Not Eat That Frog!)

So, what does this one-minute principal teach you and how does it work? In Japanese culture, the practice of Kaizen is a one-minute self-improvement principle you need to teach yourself. The center of this principle is an idea or a goal that you want to set for yourself to do. Start practicing this for 1 minute at the same time every day. This won't be difficult for anybody to do and it will make it convenient for you to incorporate this into your life with no hassle. People find it very difficult to take out 15 minutes or 30 minutes of the day but one minute will unlikely have any effect on your life.

Whether you decide to read or listen to a podcast, do it for 1 minute every day. When you begin doing this activity you may not enjoy it and you may even regret making this decision in the first place. After a few days you will realize that this seemingly unpleasant activity has started to bring you a lot of satisfaction and happiness so much that you look forward to it. The one minute you invested every day is something that you start taking seriously and this helps you to slowly but surely move towards self-discipline and this helps you to achieve better results.

When you overcome the lack of confidence, feelings of guilts or the belief that you will not be able to do something, you start moving towards a successful path and move forward. Inspiring yourself is important if you want to stay away from procrastination and feel motivated to do things on a regular basis, and that's exactly what this principle helps you to do. Once you start to enjoy spending a minute on a certain thing every day you can then start increasing the amount of time you spend on the task until you realize that you want to spend more and more time doing it because it helps you get closer to your goal. This technique is a great way to teach yourself self-discipline.

Kaizen is a principle that comes from Japan and consists of two words - Kai which means 'change' and Zen which refers to wisdom. It was invented by a philosopher known as Masaaki Imai based on his own life and it has benefitted several successful business owners.

Many people surprisingly know about The Kaizen principle, but they do not pay too much attention to it because they believe that if something asks you to invest just one minute of your time it is not going to prove to be fruitful in any way. But the truth is, when you incorporate it daily and spend a minute of your routine focusing on something, it will shape your life for the better and train yourself to be more successful. There are several benefits that Kaizen has that you should make yourself aware of.

It Helps in Waste Reduction

When you implement the principles of Kaizen it helps you to save a lot of your resources that were going down the drain and enables you to identify these unnecessary expenses in your personal as well as professional life. The technique helps you identify what benefits your business and what doesn't and how you can eliminate waste and focus on the important procedures to grow your business and save resources.

Immediate Troubleshooting

When you confront a problem sooner, you manage to resolve it a lot faster. With the one-minute rule, Kaizen helps you to resolve issues almost instantly by beginning to invest just a minute a day in trying to solve it. While it may seem like a temporary solution, within a few weeks you'll realize just how far you have come and how much you managed to overcome without even realizing the amount of effort you put in.

Optimum Utilization

The amount of time required to prioritize your needs using the Kaizen process is simple and this means that it is easy to implement irrespective of how busy your life is. You don't have to worry about dealing with too many demands or limited resources anymore because Kaizen helps you to prioritize what's important and focus on eliminating anything that is necessary in your life.

Better Teamwork

When an organization implements Kaizen in the team it helps to lift spirits, and everyone starts to work using a fresh perspective that focused on a common goal which is the growth of the business rather than their own hidden agenda. When the team works together as one, it automatically reflects in the results you see in front of you and you see your business growing much faster.

Better Quality

When you start implementing Kaizen in your business, you realize that the quality of work delivered by the employees is much better and everyone starts to work in a streamlined manner. It also helps to encourage every employee to work to their full potential and this is something you will benefit from greatly.

Another great thing about the Kaizen principle is that it works in sync with everything else we have spoken about in this book so far which includes not wasting time, unnecessary brainstorming, and meetings that don't prove to be fruitful. All you need to do is ask your employees to invest a minute of their time every day and this not only encourages them to deliver four-fold results, but it makes them more positive human beings, and this will impact the entire workforce from the lowest position to top management in the organization. You will be surprised to see how one simple change can turn the business around 180 degrees.

Chapter 11:
3 Little-Known Techniques by Top Gurus

There are three key elements that you need to keep in mind in order to avoid procrastination. There are several top industry experts that have suggestions as to how you can avoid procrastination and you need to keep these tips in mind in order to be successful at what you do. Here we will look at the three tips that you probably didn't know about and these tips or techniques will help you overcome the need to procrastinate and help you take charge of your responsibilities.

Avoid Multitasking

Multitasking is a very common technique that several people use in today to cover various job responsibilities. People usually take on more than they can handle because they want to impress, and they feel that they will be able to get that much-needed promotion by working hard. When you take on too many responsibilities you will not be able to do justice to all of them and you will end up procrastinating on the less important tasks. What this eventually does this is it creates a lot of pressure on you when the smaller tasks are done. Let us take the example of an office workspace. While your prime responsibility would be to take care of your team that reports to you and ensure that performance is up to the mark, you may end up taking more responsibilities that will help you learn more at your workspace. While learning is good, taking on extra responsibilities and attending classes to improve your skills is something that will hamper your current work. When this happens, you will start feeling frustrated and you will not pay attention to what your primary responsibilities are. You will end up being so focused on what you want to do that you forget about what you must do. Procrastination is a vicious circle and once you start delaying certain responsibilities you will end up running behind when the time comes to deliver these responsibilities.

Start Enjoying Your Work

People usually avoid doing certain tasks because they don't see it as fun. A child will unlikely want to study for his math exam if he does not enjoy learning math. Similarly, you will not end up wanting to create reports in the office because you do not really enjoy doing it. While tasks like creating reports is a very monotonous job and can take a toll on you, you need to start looking at ways you can enjoy doing these tasks. When you start doing this you will avoid procrastination and it will help you complete the task. One of the best ways to avoid procrastination is when you start having fun at work. If your responsibilities at work are not fun, then you can make it fun by involving others in your duties. When you start working in collaboration you will be able to ensure that you do justice to the job and you will no longer wait till the last minute to submit a task.

Prioritize

Prioritizing is extremely important - you need to make sure that you do not undermine a task just because it is boring or difficult to complete. As we spoke about earlier, there are ways that you can delegate your responsibilities, and this is something that you should use to your advantage. When you start prioritizing and using the 10-minute rule you will be able to complete tasks more efficiently and avoid procrastination in your personal as well as your professional life.

You need to start implementing these techniques in order to become more efficient in your daily life. While procrastination maybe the easy way out, you should know that it is not a solution and you will not be able to complete anything on time if you continue hiding behind the cloak of procrastination.

Chapter 12:
How I Stopped Procrastinating (The # 1 Method)

When you achieve productivity, the first thing that someone is going to ask you is what helped you get this productive in the first place. I have written of people's productivity and how it drastically improved in a short time frame. I depended on the Pomodoro technique, which is an effective solution to help overcome procrastination and get more productive not just at your workplace but in your personal life as well. There are different things you can try and a ton of solutions you will find when it comes to overcoming procrastination. Here is what I believe, the minute you find your rhythm and you find something that works well for you, stick to it and begin improvising your behavior based on the technique that works. It is healthy to challenge yourself from time to time, but when you already have a solution that helps you better yourself and challenge yourself at your workplace and in your personal life there is no reason for you to try another technique. Using your 10-minute goal and even the 5-second rule comes in handy in certain scenarios, but if you want to plan your life and make sure that you achieve success without compromising on quality of life, then the Pomodoro technique is something I recommend you try. This is a popular concept and it has managed to stand the test of time, making it a great effective strategy to apply. The core focus of the pomodoro technique is the 80/20 rule which you need to get accustomed to. This rule pushes you to your limits and helps you train your mind to get better with each challenge that you face.

How It Works

The Pomodoro technique was invented in the 1980's for students to study more effectively without wasting time on other activities. What initially began as a training program for students turned out to be effective for people almost across the world and in different age groups. The technique is simple and is called timeboxing. We are often in situations where we can't figure out how to start a task because it seems too overwhelming. Instead of worrying about how you are going to balance out your work, most people decide to give up even before they try because they are sure they are not going to manage to get it all done. The Pomodoro technique is basically timing yourself for 25-minute intervals.

For you to use the technique you need to first identify which task you would like to begin on and how you want to work on it. Once you have a list of tasks at hand, start by prioritizing the most important ones from the less important ones and pick out the one that you must get done today.

You can decide to break down this task into several smaller portions so that it does not overwhelm you and helps you to get the job done more efficiently.

Now you need to set your pomodoro or your timer to 25 minutes. You have to continue to challenge yourself to work for an uninterrupted 25 minutes until the timer has run out. As soon as your 25 minutes is up you give yourself a quick 5-minute break. You repeat this for at least four to five times, taking quick 5-minute breaks in between, and at the end of about 5 sessions you can take a longer break which is about 20 minutes.

It's surprising how simple this technique is and yet how effectively it works not only to help you overcome your challenges but also to take on more work and deliver effective result in no time. When you know you have just 25 minutes, your brain starts to function a lot faster and you begin rationalizing the work and delegating it more effectively so that you get it done very effectively at the end of the 25 minutes. When you set a constraint, it helps you to focus more effectively because you need to get it done before the time runs out. People who lack concentration or suffer from ADD/ADHD will find this technique very helpful and they manage to get more results out of it.

When you start using the Pomodoro technique you manage to measure your results within the very first week and see if you managed to accomplish a lot more than you set out to do at the start of the week.

The Procrastination Cure (It's Not Eat That Frog!)

When you limit yourself to a time constraint you start building momentum for the tasks you are working on and your productivity increases with confidence. You won't have time to second guess yourself because of the time constraint and this helps you put in effort into delivering quality work by paying more attention to what is required.

I am going to be honest with you, the Pomodoro technique may not seem like the easiest technique to adapt to when you first try it because the time constraints can be a little overwhelming. Your first few attempts may be failures and you may want to stop the timer midway so you can restart it and give yourself a little more time to work on the task at hand. After a few attempts, you will realize that it is quite efficient, and you will manage to divide your work effectively in two portions of 25 minutes so you can get the job done with ease as well as efficiency. 25 minutes may seem like a really small time window for you to complete a task but when you put your mind to it you will end up delivering a lot more than you would expect and you will realize that you can cover most of your work during the first half of the day.

It's a great hack to train your mind to focus without having to incorporate it into too many aspects in your life and this makes it simple to follow. All you need is a timer or an app to make it more interesting and you can start your journey to overcome procrastination and become more efficient.

The reason I recommend this technique is because people don't have too much time to plan daily and this is a simple rule that you won't have to remember. Once you find a technique that works for you, make sure you use it to your benefit and start converting all your procrastination habits into success stories one step at a time. You don't have to take big leaps and bounds and make huge changes in your life to achieve success and overcome procrastination. A small change can make a huge difference in your life so all you need to do is begin with that one change to start working towards a more positive and fruitful life.

Successful Tips to Help You Get Closer to Your Dream

Tips Used by A Billionaire

We all want to become successful and achieve the highest level of success in our career as well as in our personal life. While it's great for us to dream, it's important that we begin acting towards our goals if we want to turn them into a reality anytime soon. Nothing worth fighting for comes easy and you must put in a lot of effort and stay determined if you want to get closer to your goal. With a little effort and hard work, the more time you spend in self-discipline and following the right rules towards success. You will soon be able to see your goal and measure it at an arm's distance from you. It all begins with deciding to become successful and believing in yourself. You need to stop procrastinating and tell yourself that you are worth it, and you will achieve your goals no matter what. Once you have set that up, you can then follow these tips that will help you get closer to achieving your goal.

Follow Your Dreams

If you want to do something big you have to have big dreams. There's no harm in dreaming big about things you want to achieve, whether it's starting up a business or establishing something you are passionate about. The more you think about something the closer you will manage to get to it and this will help you to challenge yourself in believing that you have to work hard for it. It is important for you to visualize because when you visualize not only do you start relating to your dream, but it will help you to convert your dream into a goal that you aim at achieving.

You need to make sure that the goal or dream you set out to achieve is realistic. Once you figure out what you want to achieve then should give yourself a stipulated time frame and believe that you will achieve it by putting in a certain amount of hard work and staying determined.

Make A Positive Difference

If you want to feel good about yourself, you need to do something good from within. If you don't have a lot of money to do good you can practice humanitarian efforts by stepping outside to share a little money with a homeless man, buy him a meal, or even give him a blanket so he can stay warm. This may seem completely irrelevant to becoming successful, but the truth is when you share the little that you have with people who are less fortunate than you there is a warm feeling that takes over your heart and it makes you want to do better things for yourself. Feelings of gratitude are something that plays a huge role in becoming successful and every time you do something good you want to push yourself to work a little harder. Consider it karma - what goes around definitely comes around and when you do good to people, good eventually happens to you as well. Because people believe that doing good will eventually end up in a good result, they start putting in more effort towards the job that they have at hand and believe that the reason it is being done so effectively is because they are positive people. This is a cycle and once you understand your role in it you manage to smoothly balance out your life and continue to stay positive by contributing the little you can do to another people's life.

Believe in Your Ideas

When you dream big and you want to achieve your dreams you need to have a plan to achieve them. You will have to brainstorm vigorously in order to come up with an effective plan that won't fail you and will help you to get closer to your desired goal. Don't come up with 10 different plans and try them all to see which one works best. Put all your energy on focusing to create one foolproof idea that you know is so strong it won't fail you. Sometimes ideas do not come to you instantly and you need to take a while to think about how you can make your visions into a reality. Don't waste your time forcing yourself to come up with ideas. Do things that will calm you down and make you feel good because these are the things that can help you think more effectively. If there's too much going on in your head, clear your mind by going for walk or head to the beach and sit there for a while until you are ready. Think about the various scenarios where you could apply your business ideas and see whether it seems to be a profitable solution or not. 9 out of 10 times your solution is not going to be great, but the 10th time it will likely be the jackpot that you've always been waiting for and that's when your journey towards success truly begins. Think about innovation, think outside of the box, think about ideas no one has ever come up with. Strive to make a difference in people's life and plan effectively.

Connect with The People You Work With

When you have your own establishment or organization, focus on enjoying the kind of work you do and make sure that the people around you also enjoy themselves. Do not strive to be a boss from hell, those are the kind of people that don't get too far. Try to keep your employees as happy as possible because motivation is essential for them to be productive, and the more motivated they are the better assets they are to your organization. Look out for them and always treat them with kindness. When you provide a positive work environment for your employees they start delivering with their full potential and you will manage to get a strong group of people who strive to achieve your dream goal along with you. When you have multiple people working towards one goal the journey gets a lot shorter and it also gets easier.

Don't Give Up

Part of the journey of life is to experience failures - no matter how foolproof your methodologies are there going to be times when you face it alone. There will be problems in your life, but that doesn't mean you give up. It simply means you challenge yourself to work harder and you start stronger than you did with the previous attempt. Figure out what went wrong so you can come up with a solution to deal with the scenario in case it comes up again. You must accept failure as a part of your journey and consider it as one of the challenges that you need to deal with but always stay prepared. Businesses often encounter losses and while some of them find it difficult to deal with these losses and overcome obstacles there are others that take it with a grain of salt and move ahead. The only differences between the two organizations are planning and preparation, and determination to continue no matter what. When you start your own organization, you must keep yourself prepared for the worst and celebrate the success so that there is no loose end that could create problems for the business.

Set Yourself Up for New Challenges

A lot of business owners end up establishing their dream organization and this is where it ends - once they achieve that they no longer strive to move ahead or progress any further. This is probably the worst thing you can do because you stagnate your growth when you can truly do a lot more than you had initially set out to do. Every time you get close to achieving a goal, think about a new goal in life, so you aim at working towards it. The worst thing you can do to your brain is stop challenging it because that's when you no longer have anything to look forward to. You should live a life where you constantly look forward to doing something challenging and different and that's the reason why you must keep increasing your challenges and conquer your fears. Once you learn how to reach your first goal you should then look back at your experience and plan something on the lines of that but with a little more intensity. Within a few years you will realize that you have achieved a lot more than you initially set out to do and this will motivate you to help others do the same for themselves as well.

Spend Time with Your Family and Friends

One of the biggest challenges when you become an entrepreneur is lack of time. You may believe that you must compromise your personal life for you to achieve bigger and better things on your work front. You must remind yourself that nothing comes before your family and if you are not able to keep your family happy you will not be able to keep yourself happy. Always find time to spend with your family and never miss important occasions no matter what. Plan your days in advance so that you never come across a situation where you need to choose between attending your child's birthday party or attending a meeting that is crucial for your business.

Hire reliable employees whom you can delegate your work to and give yourself a little room to breathe. While you should continue working on a regular basis you need to make sure that you don't bite off more than you can chew because that is where it begins to go downhill.

Get Outside

When you have a day off don't spend it in front of the television, rather, go out and enjoy nature. Plan a picnic with your family and go on spontaneous road trips just so you can have some fun away from the indoors. You need to train your children to be self-disciplined but not forget to have fun and for you to do this you got to teach them how they can enjoy life even by being successful and making the right choices. You should transform your positive energy into teaching lessons to your children from a young age because this is what helps them follow your footsteps and learn how to work hard and achieve what they want to. At the end of the day no one remembers how many hours they spent with their family in front of the television but rather the number of memories they created on trips and holidays. If you can slip in a few days of leave with your family, you can give yourself a much-needed vacation. If you want to perform as effectively and with the same zeal that you had from the day you started your journey you must keep giving yourself breaks and reminding yourself that it is fine to have fun. Don't forget how it all started and always keep your goal in mind. The trips you take and the pampering sessions you have should all be fuel for you to accomplishing small and large goals.

Prove People Wrong

There are going to be times when you come across people who might not appreciate what you do or have something bad to say to you. Don't let that affect you. One of the major reasons why people end up procrastinating is because they take to heart what another person says and forget what they can do. If someone puts you down, do not reciprocate in a negative manner but rather take it as a little criticism and work towards proving them wrong. If you believe you can truly achieve something and there are people who tell you otherwise, don't listen to them. Trust what your heart tells you and believe in the plan you set for yourself. Believing you can achieve something is one of the most effective ways to getting it done. Do not let other people tell you what you are not capable of doing. You are the best judge of that. Make sure you work hard and let people know about your success after you have achieved it. If someone tries to put you down don't tell them what you will achieve but wait for the moment to tell them what you have achieved so you can prove them wrong with confidence. Most millionaires started off broke and with no idea what they were going to do. If they decided to quit, we wouldn't have some of the biggest industries today.

Do What You Love

Stephen N. Murphy

Just because your ideas are different from someone else's doesn't make you an odd person. It just makes you different and unique. Innovation and unique ideas are what people strive for today so when someone tells you that you are weird or unusual don't take it as criticism but consider it your uniqueness because that is what's going to help you become successful. Do crazy things in life because it will help you learn little lessons that will take you a long way. Not all your experiments are going to be successful, some may be terrible failures - but that doesn't mean you give up. It just means you must try a little harder.

If you find this book helpful in anyway a review to support my endeavors is much appreciated.

The Procrastination Cure (It's Not Eat That Frog!)

Stephen N. Murphy

www.ingramcontent.com/pod-product-compliance
Lightning Source LLC
Chambersburg PA
CBHW060614080526
44585CB00013B/830